GRANNY SQUARE CROCHET: QUILT BLOCKS

GRANNY SQUARE CROCHET: QUILT BLOCKS

36 crocheted blocks based on traditional quilting designs and 10 beautiful projects

LAURA STRUTT

CICO BOOKS

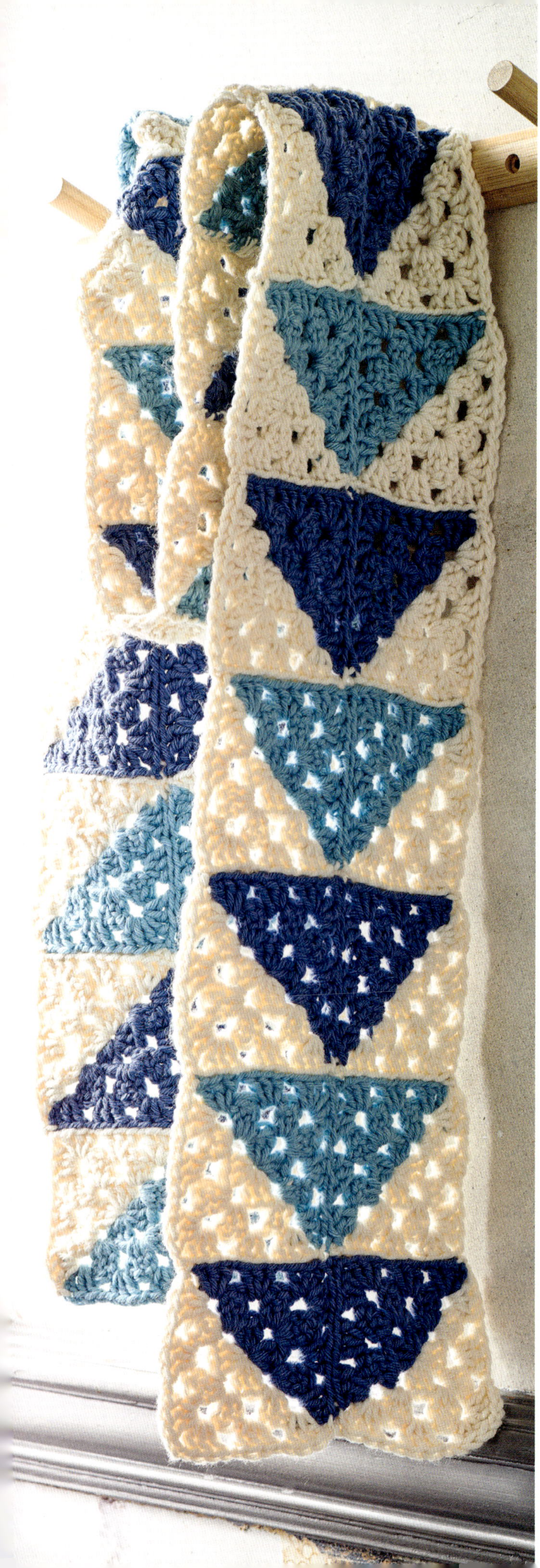

For Ethan Wolf and Elkie Raven—
no matter what.

Published in 2026 by CICO Books
an imprint of Ryland Peters & Small Ltd
1452 Davis Bugg Road, Warrenton, NC 27589
www.rylandpeters.com

10 9 8 7 6 5 4 3 2 1

US Library of Congress CIP data has been applied for.

ISBN: 978 1 80065 593 5

Printed in China

Editor: Marie Clayton
Pattern checker: Carol Ibbetson
Designer: Alison Fenton
Photographer: James Gardiner
Stylist: Nel Haynes
Illustrator: Stephen Dew

In-house editor: Jenny Dye
Art director: Sally Powell
Creative director: Leslie Harrington
Production manager: Gordana Simakovic
Publishing manager: Carmel Edmonds

CONTENTS

INTRODUCTION

The first thing I ever learned to crochet was a granny square, and while my crochet journey has since grown to include larger projects, garments, and amigurumi, I always find myself drawn back to the humble granny square. There's something timeless, comforting and endlessly versatile about it. It's a design that welcomes beginners and still manages to surprise and inspire seasoned crocheters. For me, it's the foundation of so many creative possibilities.

This book brings together my love of crochet and my longtime fascination with patchwork. I've always been captivated by the bold graphics and carefully balanced color stories in traditional quilts, and this collection explores how those same principles can be translated into yarn. Inspired by both classic quilting motifs and more modern interpretations, these crochet blocks reimagine familiar shapes—like hexagons, diamonds, stars, and pinwheels—through stitches, texture, and color.

The patterns in this book are also incredibly customizable. By changing the yarn weight or hook size, you can adjust the finished size and style of the blocks to suit whatever you're making—whether it's a bold throw, a patchwork-style cardigan, a pillow cover, or a small bag. Some blocks are simple and meditative, others offer a more technical challenge, but all are designed to be fun and rewarding to make.

Whether you're a beginner exploring granny squares for the first time or an experienced crocheter looking for fresh ideas, I hope this collection inspires you to play and experiment and enjoy the creative possibilities of patchwork-inspired crochet.

BEFORE YOU BEGIN

THE BLOCKS

The majority of the blocks are worked in rounds, turning at the end of each round, so that the wrong side is uppermost on alternate rounds. This helps the squares lay flatter pre-blocking (see page 124).

There are three types of blocks in this book. The first are the basic blocks, which can be used as a background, as part of a larger design, or incorporated into a bigger block.

The second type are the seamed blocks. These are made up of multiple smaller blocks arranged in a pattern and joined together with an invisible seam to create one larger block.

Finally, the third type are the colorwork blocks. These blocks use different colors for various sections—for example, the Circle in a Square/ Drunkard's Path, where each section is worked in a different color.

TRADITIONAL VS SOLID GRANNY SQUARES

Traditional granny square

Solid granny square

A traditional granny square is made with clusters of stitches separated by chain spaces, giving it a lacy, open look. It's worked in rounds from the center, with gaps that make it lightweight and breathable. This makes it perfect for throws and shawls.

A solid granny square, on the other hand, has stitches worked tightly together with no gaps. This makes it denser and sturdier. Also worked in rounds, it creates a thicker, warmer fabric ideal for bags, pot holder, or cozy throws.

In short, traditional granny squares are airy and open, while solid granny squares are dense and solid.

For many of the blocks and projects in this book, you can choose to work with either a solid granny square or a traditional granny square, depending on your preference. Solid granny squares produce a denser fabric, so garments and throws might feel cozier but will be less breathable than those made with traditional granny squares.

YARN

Each block is made using light worsted (DK) weight yarn and a US size G-6 (4mm) hook. I've chosen Stylecraft Special DK for the blocks because of its excellent stitch definition and huge range of colors. The measurements of each block are based on this yarn and hook size, so bear in mind that the measurements of your block will change if you use yarn in a different weight.

USING COLOR

Using a yarn such as Stylecraft Special DK, which has a large range of colors, makes it easy to experiment with different palettes and effects, whether you're drawn to rich contrasts, gentle neutrals, or playful brights. Color plays a huge role in how these blocks look and feel. Value—how light or dark a color is—can be just as important as the shade itself. High-contrast combinations highlight shapes and structure, while lower-contrast pairings create softer, more blended results. Drawing on a few basic principles of color theory can help you make choices that add harmony, movement, or drama to your work.

CUSTOMIZING THE PROJECTS

Taking blocks further, you can use the suggested blocks in the projects or get creative with your own designs. If you swap blocks, be sure to check the number of rounds the block has and make sure your chosen block can be worked to the right size. Also, check how many blocks are needed. If you want to swap a motif in a throw, pick a block made up of the same number of squares to ensure a neat fit.

SKILL LEVELS

If you are new to crochet, turn to the Techniques section on pages 114–125 and the Abbreviations on page 127. The stitch names and abbreviations used in this book are the US versions—turn to page 127 for the equivalent UK terms. Start with the basic blocks in chapter 1 and then move on to the seamed and colorwork blocks and the projects once you know the basic techniques. Each project also has a skill rating, from Easy (one circle) to Intermediate (two circles) and Advanced (three circles).

Chapter 1

BASIC BLOCKS

1 PLAIN SQUARE

This clean, uninterrupted square is often used to showcase bold color, texture, or print—it's the simplest and most versatile building block in quilt style design. These blocks can be made in both the solid and the traditional granny square style and can be worked in a single color or variegated, patterned, and hand-painted yarns.

VERSION A: **CLASSIC GRANNY SQUARE**

(Single color with turns)

Make a magic ring.
Round 1 (RS): Working into ring, ch3 (counts as 1dc throughout), 2dc, ch2, [3dc, ch2] 3 times, join with sl st to top of beg ch-3, turn. (*4 dc clusters, separated by ch-2 corners*)
Round 2 (WS): Sl st in corner sp, (ch3, 2dc, ch1) in same corner sp, [(3dc, ch2, 3dc, ch1) in next corner sp] 3 times, (3dc, ch2) in last corner sp, join with sl st to top of beg ch-3, turn.
Round 3 (RS): Sl st in corner sp, (ch3, 2dc, ch1) in same corner sp, [3dc in next ch sp, ch1, (3dc, ch2, 3dc, ch1) in next corner sp] 3 times, 3dc in next ch sp, ch1, (3dc, ch2) in last corner sp, join with sl st to top of beg ch-3, turn.
Round 4 (WS): Sl st in corner sp, (ch3, 2 dc, ch1) in same corner sp, *[3dc in next ch sp, ch1] twice, (3dc, ch2, 3dc, ch1) in next corner sp; rep from * twice more, [3dc in next ch sp, ch1] twice, (3dc, ch2) in last corner sp, join with sl st to top of beg ch-3.
Fasten off.

YOU WILL NEED

Crochet hook

Yarn in one color:
Green

Yarn needle

FINISHED MEASUREMENTS

4 x 4in (10 x 10cm)

ABBREVIATIONS

beg - beginning
ch - chain
dc - double crochet
rep - repeat
RS - right side
sl st - slip stitch
sp - space
st(s) - stitch(es)
WS - wrong side

( ) - stitch sequences within round brackets are worked into the same stitch or space stated
[ ] - stitch sequences within square brackets are worked the number of times stated
* - repeat sequence from * number of times stated

VERSION B: **SOLID GRANNY SQUARE**

(Single color with turns)

Make a magic ring.

Round 1 (RS): Working into ring, ch3 (counts as 1dc throughout), 2dc, ch2, [3dc, ch2] 3 times, join with sl st to top of beg ch-3, turn. (*4 dc clusters, separated by ch-2 corners*)

Round 2 (WS): Sl st in corner sp, (ch3, 1dc) in same corner sp, 1dc in next 3 sts, [(2dc, ch2, 2dc) in next corner sp, 1dc in next 3 sts] 3 times, (2dc, ch2) in last corner sp, join with sl st to top of beg ch-3, turn.

Round 3 (RS): Sl st in corner sp, (ch3, 1dc) in same corner sp, 1dc in next 7 sts, [(2dc, ch2, 2dc) in next corner sp, 1dc in next 7 sts] 3 times, (2dc, ch2) in last corner sp, join with sl st to top of beg ch-3, turn.

Round 4 (WS): Sl st in corner sp, (ch3, 1dc) in same corner sp, 1dc in next 11 sts, [(2dc, ch2, 2dc) in next corner sp, 1dc in next 11 sts] 3 times, (2dc, ch2) in last corner sp, join with sl st to top of beg ch-3.

Fasten off.

2 HALF SQUARE TRIANGLE (HST)

This is a classic unit, made from two right-angled triangles joined along the diagonal, and loved for its symmetry and endless design potential in both traditional and modern quilts. Here it is created by working with yarns of two different colors and making the changes at the diagonal points.

VERSION A: **CLASSIC GRANNY SQUARE**

(Two colors with turns)

Using A, make a magic ring.
Round 1 (RS): Working into ring, ch3 (counts as 1dc throughout), 2dc, ch2, 3dc, change to B, ch2, [3dc, ch2] twice more, join with sl st to top of beg ch-3, turn. (*4 dc clusters, separated by ch-2 corners*)
Round 2 (WS): Cont in B, sl st in corner sp, (ch3, 2dc, ch1) in same corner sp, (3dc, ch2, 3dc) in next corner sp, ch1, (3dc, change to A, ch2) in next corner sp, (3dc, ch1) in same corner sp, (3dc, ch2, 3dc) in next corner sp, ch1, (3dc, ch2) in last corner sp, join with sl st to top of beg ch-3, turn.
Round 3 (RS): Cont in A, sl st in corner sp, (ch3, 2dc, ch1) in same corner sp, 3dc in next ch sp, ch1, (3dc, ch2, 3dc) in next corner sp, ch1, 3dc in next ch sp, ch1, (3dc, change to B, ch2, 3dc) in next corner sp, ch1, 3dc in next ch sp, ch1, (3dc, ch2, 3dc) in next corner sp, ch1, 3dc in next ch sp, ch1, (3dc, ch2) in last corner sp, join with sl st to top of beg ch-3, turn.
Round 4 (WS): Cont in B, sl st in corner sp, (ch3, 2dc, ch1) in same corner sp, [3dc in next ch sp, ch1] twice, (3dc, ch2, 3dc) in next corner sp, ch1, [3dc in next ch sp, ch1] twice, (3dc, change to A, ch2, 3dc) in next corner sp, ch1, [3dc in next ch sp, ch1] twice, (3dc, ch2, 3dc) in next corner sp, ch1, [3dc in next ch sp, ch1] twice, (3dc, ch2) in last corner sp, join with sl st to top of beg ch-3.
Fasten off.

YOU WILL NEED

Crochet hook

Yarn in two colors:
- Red (A)
- Purple (B)

Yarn needle

FINISHED MEASUREMENTS

4 x 4in (10 x 10cm)

ABBREVIATIONS

beg – beginning
ch – chain
cont – continu(e)ing
dc – double crochet
RS – right side
sl st – slip stitch
sp – space
st(s) – stitch(es)
WS – wrong side

( ) – stitch sequences within round brackets are worked into the same stitch or space stated
[ ] – stitch sequences within square brackets are worked the number of times stated

VERSION B: **SOLID GRANNY SQUARE**

(Two colors with turns)

Using A, make a magic ring.

Round 1 (RS): Working into ring, ch3 (counts as 1dc throughout), 2dc, ch2, 3dc, change to B, ch2, [3dc, ch2] twice more, join with sl st to top of beg ch-3, turn. (*4 dc clusters, separated by ch-2 corners*)

Round 2 (WS): Cont in B, sl st in corner sp, (ch3, 1dc) in same corner sp, 1dc in next 3 sts, (2dc, ch2, 2dc) in next corner sp, 1dc in next 3 sts, (2dc, change to A, ch2, 2dc) in next corner sp, 1dc in next 3 sts, (2dc, ch2, 2dc) in next corner sp, 1dc in next 3 sts, (2dc, ch2) in last corner sp, join with sl st to top of beg ch-3, turn.

Round 3 (RS): Cont in A, sl st in corner sp, (ch3, 1dc) in same corner sp, 1dc in next 7 sts, (2dc, ch2, 2dc) in next corner sp, 1dc in next 7 sts, (2dc, change to B, ch2, 2dc) in next corner sp, 1dc in next 7 sts, (2dc, ch2, 2dc) in next corner sp, 1dc in next 7 sts, (2dc, ch2) in last corner, join with sl st to top of beg ch-3, turn.

Round 4 (WS): Cont in B, sl st in corner sp, (ch3, 1dc) in same corner sp, 1dc in next 11 sts, (2dc, ch2, 2dc) in next corner sp, 1dc in next 11 sts, (2dc, change to A, ch2, 2dc) in next corner sp, 1dc in next 11 sts, (2dc, ch2, 2dc) in next corner sp, 1dc in next 11 sts, (2dc, ch2) in last corner sp, join with sl st to top of beg ch-3.

Fasten off.

3 SPLIT QUARTER SQUARE TRIANGLE (SQST)

In this dynamic variation of the Quarter Square Triangle, a square is divided into three segments—perfect for creating movement and layered geometry in patchwork-inspired designs.

VERSION A: **CLASSIC GRANNY SQUARE**

(Three colors with turns)

Using A, make a magic ring.
Round 1 (RS): Working into ring, ch3 (counts as 1dc throughout), 2dc, ch2, 3dc, change to B, ch2, 3dc, change to C, ch2, 3dc, ch2, join with sl st to top of beg ch-3, turn. (*4 dc clusters, separated by ch-2 corners*)
Round 2 (WS): Cont in C, sl st in corner sp, (ch3, 2dc, ch1) in same corner sp, (3dc, change to B, ch2, 3dc) in next corner sp, ch1, (3dc, change to A, ch2, 3dc) in next corner sp, ch1, (3dc, ch2, 3dc) in next corner sp, ch1, (3dc, ch2) in last corner sp, join with sl st to top of beg ch-3, turn.
Round 3 (RS): Cont in A, sl st in corner sp, (ch3, 2dc, ch1) in same corner sp, 3dc in next ch sp, ch1, (3dc, ch2, 3dc) in next corner sp, ch1, 3dc in next ch sp, ch1, (3dc, change to B, ch2, 3dc) in next corner sp, ch1, 3dc in next ch sp, ch1, (3dc, change to C, ch2, 3dc) in next corner sp, ch1, 3dc in next ch sp, ch1, (3dc, ch2) in last corner sp, join with sl st to top of beg ch-3, turn.
Round 4 (WS): Cont in C, sl st in corner sp, (ch3, 2dc, ch1) in same corner sp, [3dc in next ch sp, ch1] twice, (3dc, change to B, ch2, 3dc) in next corner sp, ch1, [3dc in next ch sp, ch1] twice, (3dc, change to A, ch2, 3dc) in next corner sp, ch1, [3dc in next ch sp, ch1] twice, (3dc, ch2, 3dc) in next corner sp, ch1, [3dc in next ch sp, ch1] twice, (3dc, ch2) in last corner sp, join with sl st to top of beg ch-3.
Fasten off.

YOU WILL NEED

Crochet hook

Yarn in three colors:
- Blue (A)
- Cream (B)
- Teal (C)

Yarn needle

FINISHED MEASUREMENTS

4 x 4in (10 x 10cm)

ABBREVIATIONS

beg - beginning
ch - chain
cont - continu(e)ing
dc - double crochet
RS - right side
sl st - slip stitch
sp - space
st(s) - stitch(es)
WS - wrong side

( ) - stitch sequences within round brackets are worked into the same stitch or space stated
[ ] - stitch sequences within square brackets are worked the number of times stated

VERSION B: **SOLID GRANNY SQUARE**

(Three colors with turns)

Using A, make a magic ring.

Round 1 (RS): Working into ring, ch3 (counts as 1dc throughout), 2dc, ch2, 3dc, change to B, ch2, 3dc, change to C, ch2, 3dc, ch2, join with sl st to top of beg ch-3, turn. *(4 dc clusters, separated by ch-2 corners)*

Round 2 (WS): Cont in C, sl st in corner sp, (ch3, 1dc) in same corner sp, 1dc in next 3 sts, (2dc, change to B, ch2, 2dc) in next corner sp, 1dc in next 3 sts, (2dc, change to A, ch2, 2dc) in next corner sp, 1dc in next 3 sts, (2dc, ch2, 2dc) in next corner sp, 1dc in next 3 sts, (2dc, ch2) in last corner sp, join with sl st to top of beg ch-3, turn.

Round 3 (RS): Cont in A, sl st in corner sp, (ch3, 1dc) in same corner sp, 1dc in next 7 sts, (2dc, ch2, 2dc) in next corner sp, 1dc in next 7 sts, (2dc, change to B, ch2, 2dc) in next corner sp, 1dc in next 7 sts, (2dc, change to C, ch2, 2dc) in next corner sp, 1dc in next 7 sts, (2dc, ch2) in last corner sp, join with sl st to top of beg ch-3, turn.

Round 4 (WS): Cont in C, sl st in corner sp, (ch3, 1dc) in same corner sp, 1dc in next 11 sts, (2dc, change to B, ch2, 2dc) in next corner sp, 1dc in next 11 sts, (2dc, change to A, ch2, 2dc) in next corner sp, 1dc in next 11 sts, (2dc, ch2, 2dc) in next corner sp, 1dc in next 11 sts, (2dc, ch2) in last corner sp, join with sl st to top of beg ch-3. Fasten off.

4 QUARTER SQUARE TRIANGLE (QST)

Formed from four right-angled triangles meeting at the center, this block is great for adding symmetry in designs and it is frequently seen in quilt design—both modern and traditional—for Card Trick blocks (see page 35) and Hourglass motifs.

VERSION A: **CLASSIC GRANNY SQUARE**

(Four colors with turns)

Using A, make a magic ring.

Round 1 (RS): Working into ring, ch3 (counts as 1dc throughout), 2dc, change to B, ch2, 3dc, change to C, ch2, 3dc, change to D, ch2, 3dc, join with sl st to top of beg ch-3, turn. (*4 dc clusters, separated by ch-2 corners*)

Round 2 (WS): Cont in D, sl st in corner sp, (ch3, 2dc, ch1) in same corner sp, (3dc, change to C, ch2, 3dc) in next corner sp, ch1, (3dc, change to B, ch2, 3dc) in next corner sp, ch1, (3dc, change to A, ch2, 3dc) in next corner sp, ch1, (3dc, ch2) in last corner sp, join with sl st to top of beg ch-3, turn.

Round 3 (RS): Cont in A, sl st in corner sp, (ch3, 2dc, ch1) in same corner sp, 3dc in next ch sp, ch1, (3dc, change to B, ch2, 3dc) in next corner sp, ch1, 3dc in next ch sp, ch1, (3dc, change to C, ch2, 3dc) in next corner sp, ch1, 3dc in next ch sp, ch1, (3dc, change to D, ch2, 3dc) in next corner sp, ch1, 3dc in next ch sp, ch1, (3dc, ch2) in last corner sp, join with sl st to top of beg ch-3, turn.

Round 4 (WS): Cont in D, sl st in corner sp, (ch3, 2dc, ch1) in same corner sp, [3dc in next ch sp, ch1] twice, (3dc, change to C, ch2, 3dc) in next corner sp, ch1, [3dc in next ch sp, ch1] twice, (3dc, change to B, ch2, 3dc) in next corner sp, ch1, [3dc in next ch sp, ch1] twice, (3dc, change to A, ch2, 3dc) in next corner sp, ch1, [3dc in next ch sp, ch1] twice, (3dc, ch2) in last corner sp, join with sl st to top of beg ch-3.

Fasten off.

YOU WILL NEED

Crochet hook

Yarn in four colors:
- Cream (A)
- Red (B)
- Cream (C)
- Pink (D)

Yarn needle

FINISHED MEASUREMENTS

4 x 4in (10 x 10cm)

ABBREVIATIONS

beg - beginning
ch - chain
cont - continu(e)ing
dc - double crochet
RS - right side
sl st - slip stitch
sp - space
st(s) - stitch(es)
WS - wrong side

( ) - stitch sequences within round brackets are worked into the same stitch or space stated
[ ] - stitch sequences within square brackets are worked the number of times stated

VERSION B: **SOLID GRANNY SQUARE**

(Four colors with turns)

Using A, make a magic ring.
Round 1 (RS): Working into ring, ch3 (counts as 1dc throughout), 2dc, change to B, ch2, 3dc, change to C, ch2, 3dc, change to D, ch2, 3dc, join with sl st to top of beg ch-3, turn. (*4 dc clusters, separated by ch-2 corners*)
Round 2 (WS): Cont in D, sl st in corner sp, ch3, 1dc in same corner sp, 1dc in next 3 sts, (2dc, change to C, ch2, 2dc) in next corner sp, 1dc in next 3 sts, (2dc, change to B, ch2, 2dc) in next corner sp, 1dc in next 3 sts, (2dc, change to A, ch2, 2dc) in next corner sp, 1dc in next 3 sts, (2dc, ch2) in last corner sp, join with sl st to top of beg ch-3, turn.
Round 3 (RS): Cont in A, sl st in corner sp, ch3, 1dc in same corner sp, 1dc in next 7 sts, (2dc, change to B, ch2, 2dc) in next corner sp, 1dc in next 7 sts, (2dc, change to C, ch2, 2dc) in next corner sp, 1dc in next 7 sts, (2dc, change to D, ch2, 2dc) in next corner sp, 1dc in next 7 sts, (2dc, ch2) in last corner sp, join with sl st to top of beg ch-3, turn.
Round 4 (WS): Cont in D, sl st in corner sp, ch3, 1dc in same corner sp, 1dc in next 11 sts, (2dc, change to C, ch2, 2dc) in next corner sp, 1dc in next 11 sts, (2dc, change to B, ch2, 2dc) in next corner sp, 1dc in next 11 sts, (2dc, change to A, ch2, 2dc) in next corner sp, 1dc in next 11 sts, (2dc, ch2) in last corner sp, join with sl st to top of beg ch-3.
Fasten off.

5 RECTANGLE

(Two colors per round, horizontal halves)

A square made up of two rectangles—here created with colorwork—is a simple yet very effective block to add to your design arsenal, great for creating repeated patterns or borders, or as part of a larger block like the Churn Dash (see page 37).

YOU WILL NEED

Crochet hook

Yarn in two colors:
- **Green (A)**
- **Orange (B)**

Yarn needle

FINISHED MEASUREMENTS

5 x 5in (13 x 13cm)

Using A, make a magic ring.

Round 1 (RS): Working into ring, ch3 (counts as 1dc throughout), 1dc, 1tr, 4dc, 1tr, 2dc, change to B, 2dc, 1tr, 4dc, 1tr, 2dc, join with sl st to top of beg ch-3, turn.

Round 2 (WS): Cont in B, ch3, 1dc, (2tr, 1tr, 2dc) in next st, 1dc in next 4 sts, (2dc, 1tr, 2dc) in next st, 1dc in next 2 sts, change to A, 1dc in next 2 sts, (2dc, 1tr, 2dc) in next st, 1dc in next 4 sts, (2dc, 1tr, 2dc) in next st, 1dc in next 2 sts, join with sl st to top of beg ch-3, turn.

Round 3 (RS): Cont in A, ch3, 1dc in next 3 sts, (2dc, 1tr, 2dc) in next st, 1dc in next 8 sts, (2dc, 1tr, 2dc) in next st, 1dc in next 4 sts, change to B, 1dc in next 4 sts, (2dc, 1tr, 2dc) in next st, 1dc in next 8 sts, (2dc, 1tr, 2dc) in next st, 1dc in next 4 sts, join with sl st to top of beg ch-3, turn.

Round 4 (WS): Cont in B, ch3, 1dc in next 5 sts, (2dc, 1tr, 2dc) in next st, 1dc in next 12 sts, (2dc, 1tr, 2dc) in next st, 1dc in next 6 sts, change to A, 1dc in next 6 sts, (2dc, 1tr, 2dc) in next st, 1dc in next 12 sts, (2dc, 1tr, 2dc) in next st, 1 dc in next 6 sts, join with sl st to top of beg ch-3, turn.

Round 5 (RS): Cont in A, ch3, 1dc in next 7 sts, (2dc, 1tr, 2dc) in next st, 1dc in next 16 sts, (2dc, 1tr, 2dc) in next st, 1dc in next 8 sts, change to B, 1dc in next 8 sts, (2dc, 1tr, 2dc) in next st, 1dc in next 16 sts, (2dc, 1tr, 2dc) in next st, 1dc in next 8 sts, join with sl st to top of beg ch-3.

Fasten off.

TIP

Yarn color choice is key to how your design will look. For bold, defined patterns, choose colors with strong contrast. For a softer look, go with similar tones. Lay your yarns side by side before starting. If they blur together, the block may be lost in the finished piece.

ABBREVIATIONS

beg – beginning
ch – chain
cont – continu(e)ing
dc – double crochet
RS – right side
sl st – slip stitch
sp – space
st(s) – stitch(es)
tr – treble crochet
WS – wrong side
( ) – stitch sequences within round brackets are worked into the same stitch or space stated

6 COLORWORK FOUR PATCH

(Four color changes per round with turns)

One of the simplest style blocks, this grid of four equal squares is not only beginner-friendly but also a great way to add contrast to designs. This example is made using colorwork, but you can also make a Four Patch block by seaming four squares together (see page 26).

YOU WILL NEED

Crochet hook

Yarn in four colors:
- **Red (A)**
- **Green (B)**
- **Lavender (C)**
- **Blue (D)**

Yarn needle

FINISHED MEASUREMENTS

5 x 5in (12.5 x 12.5cm)

Change color when you reach the middle of each side. Turn your work at the end of each round.

Using A, make a magic ring.

Round 1 (RS): Working into ring, ch3 (counts as 1dc throughout), 1dc, 1tr, 2dc, change to B, 2dc, 1tr, 2dc, change to C, 2dc, 1tr, 2dc, change to D, 2dc, 1tr, 2dc, join with sl st to top of beg ch-3, turn.

Round 2 (WS): Cont in D, ch3, 1dc, (2dc, 1tr, 2dc) in next st, 1dc in next 2 sts, change to C, 1dc in next 2 sts, (2dc, 1tr, 2dc) in next st, 1dc in next 2 sts, change to B, 1dc in next 2 sts, (2dc, 1tr, 2dc) in next st, 1dc in next 2 sts, change to A, 1dc in next 2 sts, (2dc, 1tr, 2dc) in next st, 1dc in next 2 sts, join with sl st to top of beg ch-3, turn.

Round 3 (RS): Cont in A, ch3, 1dc in next 3 sts, (2dc, 1tr, 2dc) in next st, 1dc in next 4 sts, change to B, 1dc in next 4 sts, (2dc, 1tr, 2dc) in next st, 1dc in next 4 sts, change to C, 1dc in next 4 sts, (2dc, 1tr, 2dc) in next st, 1dc in next 4 sts, change to D, 1dc in next 4 sts, (2dc, 1tr, 2dc) in next st, 1dc in next 4 sts, join with sl st to top of beg ch-3, turn.

Round 4 (WS): Cont in D, ch3, 1dc in next 5 sts, (2dc, 1tr, 2dc) in next st, 1dc in next 6 sts, change to C, 1dc in next 6 sts, (2dc, 1tr, 2dc) in next st, 1dc in next 6 sts, change to B, 1dc in next 6 sts, (2dc, 1tr, 2dc) in next st, 1dc in next 6 sts, change to A, 1dc in next 6 sts, (2dc, 1tr, 2dc) in next st, 1dc in next 6 sts, join with sl st to top of beg ch-3, turn.

Round 5 (RS): Cont in A, ch3, 1dc in next 7 sts, (2dc, 1tr, 2dc) in next st, 1dc in next 8 sts, change to B, 1dc in next 8 sts, (2dc, 1tr, 2dc) in next st, 1dc in next 8 sts, change to C, 1dc in next 8 sts, (2dc, 1tr, 2dc) in next st, 1dc in next 8 sts, change to D, 1dc in next 8 sts, (2dc, 1tr, 2dc) in next st, 1dc in next 8 sts, join with sl st to top of beg ch-3.

Fasten off.

ABBREVIATIONS

beg – beginning
ch – chain
cont – continu(e)ing
dc – double crochet
RS – right side
sl st – slip stitch
sp – space
st(s) – stitch(es)
tr – treble
WS – wrong side
( ) – stitch sequences within round brackets are worked into the same stitch or space stated

Chapter 2

SEAMED BLOCKS

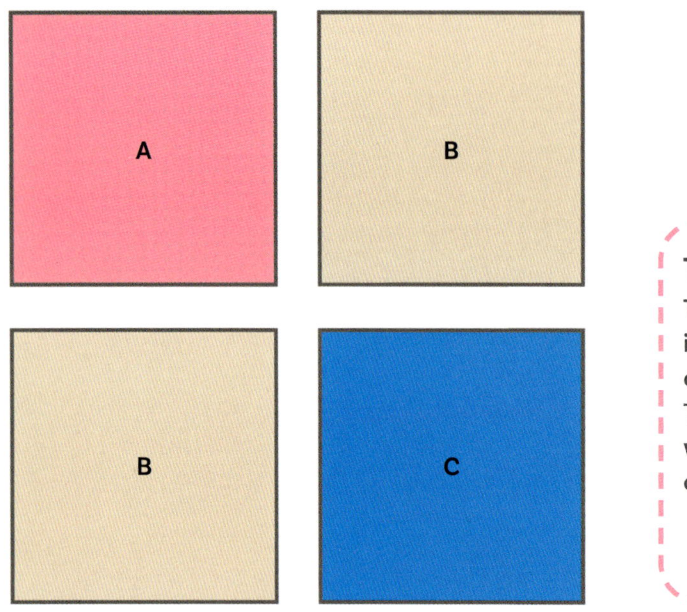

TIP
This design can be made in either the solid or the classic granny square style. To make a smaller block, work fewer rounds on each of the individual squares.

7 SEAMED FOUR PATCH

This is one of the simplest blocks, a grid of four equal squares. It's not only beginner-friendly but also a great way to add contrast to designs. This example can be made using one of two methods: seaming four squares together as here; or made in one piece using colorwork to create the design (see page 22).

YOU WILL NEED

Crochet hook and yarn in three colors (see Yarn on page 9)
- **Beige (A)**
- **Pink (B)**
- **Blue (C)**

Yarn needle

FINISHED MEASUREMENTS

5½ x 5½in (14 x 14cm)

Step 1: Create four 3-round blocks as per Block 1 Plain Square (see page 12): two using A, one using B, and one using C.

Step 2: Place the blocks in a 2 x 2 square as shown in the diagram.

Step 3: Seam together with a yarn needle and A using invisible seam technique (see page 125), first joining the vertical seams, then the horizontal seams. Weave in all ends and block as desired (see page 124).

Classic Granny Square version

Solid Granny Square version

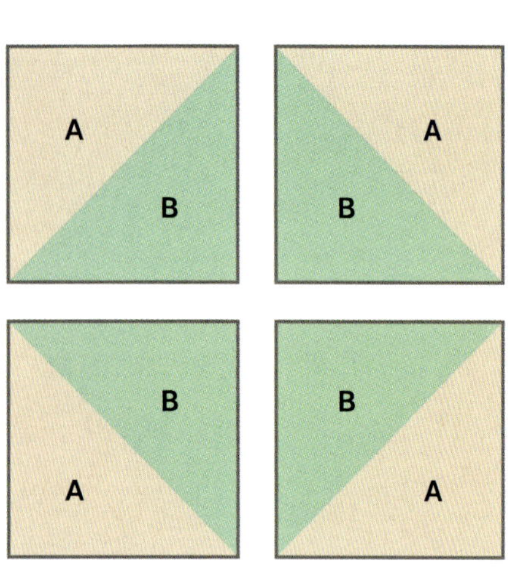

8 SEAMED DIAMOND IN A SQUARE

This bold and graphic block features Half Square Triangles (HSTs) arranged to form a diamond motif within a four-patch layout. The strong central shape adds depth and direction to your crochet patchwork. For a colorwork version of this block, see page 70.

YOU WILL NEED

Crochet hook and yarn in two colors (see Yarn on page 9)
- **Beige (A)**
- **Green (B)**

Yarn needle

FINISHED MEASUREMENTS

5¾ x 5¾in (15 x 15cm)

Step 1: Make 4 x 3-round blocks as per Block 2 Half Square Triangle (see page 14), using A & B.

Step 2: Weave in all ends (see page 124) and arrange the blocks in a 2 x 2 square as shown in the diagram.

Step 3: Seam together with a yarn needle and A using the invisible seam technique (see page 125), first joining the vertical seams, then the horizontal seams. Weave in all ends and block as desired (see page 124).

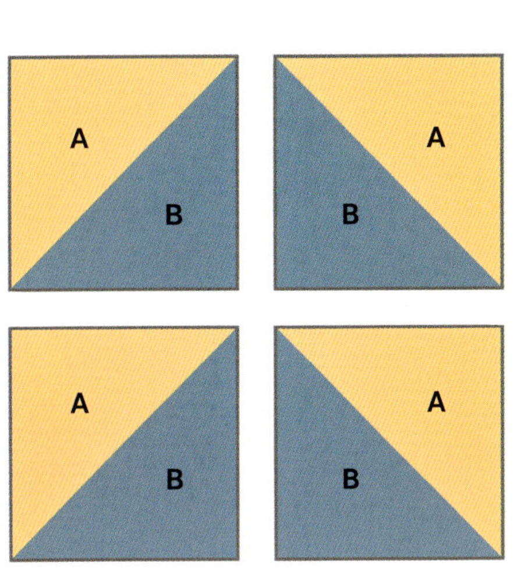

9 FLYING GEESE

Here, a bold triangle is flanked by two smaller ones, forming a directional unit. It is traditionally used in borders and to create movement across a design. The block is worked by creating four HST blocks and seaming to create the central motif.

YOU WILL NEED

Crochet hook and yarn in two colors (see Yarn on page 9)
- **Yellow (A)**
- **Blue (B)**

Yarn needle

FINISHED MEASUREMENTS

5¾ x 5¾in (15 x 15cm)

Step 1: Make 4 x 4-round blocks as per Block 2 Half Square Triangle (see page 14), using A & B.

Step 2: Place the blocks in a 2 x 2 square as shown in the diagram.

Step 3: Seam together with a yarn needle and B using the invisible seam technique (see page 125), first by joining the vertical seams, then the horizontal seams. Weave in all ends and block as desired (see page 124).

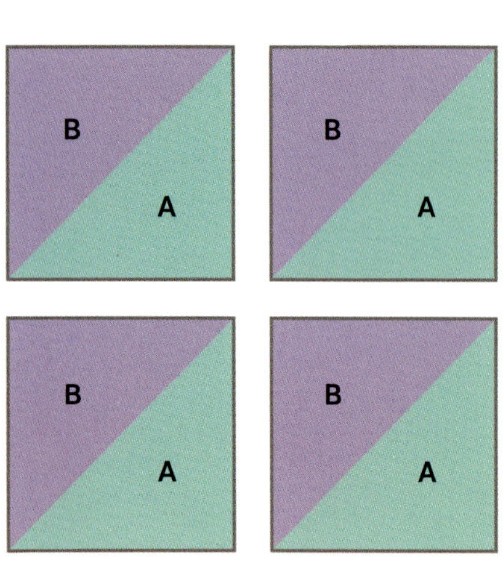

10 DIRECTIONAL HALF SQUARE TRIANGLE

This modern take on the Four Patch uses directional Half Square Triangles (HSTs) to create dynamic movement across the block. It is great for adding flow and energy to your overall design.

YOU WILL NEED

Crochet hook and yarn in two colors (see Yarn on page 9)
- **Green (A)**
- **Purple (B)**

Yarn needle

FINISHED MEASUREMENTS

5¾ x 5¾in (15 x 15cm)

Step 1: Make 4 x 3-round blocks as per Block 2 Half Square Triangle (see page 14), using A & B.

Step 2: Weave in all ends (see page 124) and arrange the blocks in a 2 x 2 square as shown in the diagram.

Step 3: Seam together with a yarn needle and A using the invisible seam technique (see page 125), first joining the vertical seams, then the horizontal seams. Weave in all ends and block as desired (see page 124).

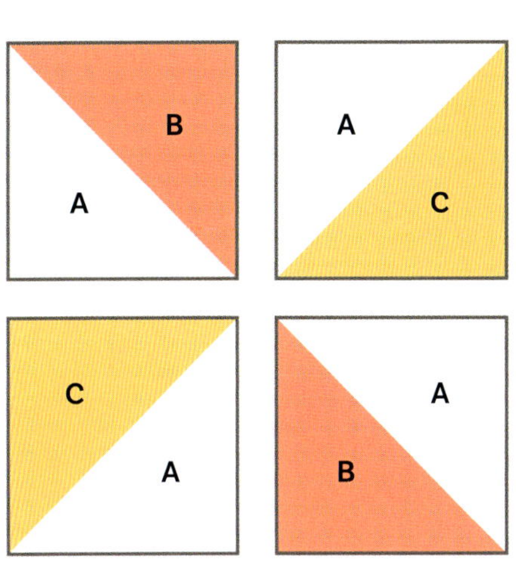

11 PINWHEEL

This block is made up of four HSTs spinning from the center like a windmill—when worked with one color for the background (A) and two colors for the accents (B and C), they can be positioned alternately to give the sense of motion in the design.

YOU WILL NEED

Crochet hook and yarn in three colors (see Yarn on page 9)
- **Cream (A)**
- **Orange (B)**
- **Yellow (C)**

Yarn needle

FINISHED MEASUREMENTS

5½ x 5½in (14 x 14cm)

Step 1: Make 4 x 4-round blocks as per Block 2 Half Square Triangle (see page 14), with 2 in B & C and 2 in A & C.

Step 2: Weave in all ends (see page 124) and arrange the blocks in a 2 x 2 square as shown in the diagram.

Step 3: Seam together with a yarn needle and B using the invisible seam technique (see page 125), first joining the vertical seams, then the horizontal seams. Weave in all ends and block as desired (see page 124).

12 DOUBLE PINWHEEL

This is a really dynamic block made from four Split Quarter Square Triangle blocks, forming a spinning double-blade effect. Similar to the traditional pinwheel designs, it adds lots of angles and the appearance of complex motion for an intricate visual effect.

YOU WILL NEED

Crochet hook and yarn in three colors (see Yarn on page 9)
- **Dark blue (A)**
- **Light Blue (B)**
- **Cream (C)**

Yarn needle

FINISHED MEASUREMENTS

5½ x 5½in (14 x 14cm)

Step 1: Make 4 x 4-round blocks as per Block 3 Split Quarter Square Triangle (see page 16), using A, B, & C and working with B and C in alternate positions.

Step 2: Place the blocks in a 2 x 2 square with one of each color in each row diagonally opposite each other, as shown in the diagram.

Step 3: Seam together with a yarn needle and using the invisible seam technique (see page 125), first joining the vertical seams, then the horizontal seams. Weave in all ends and block as desired (see page 124).

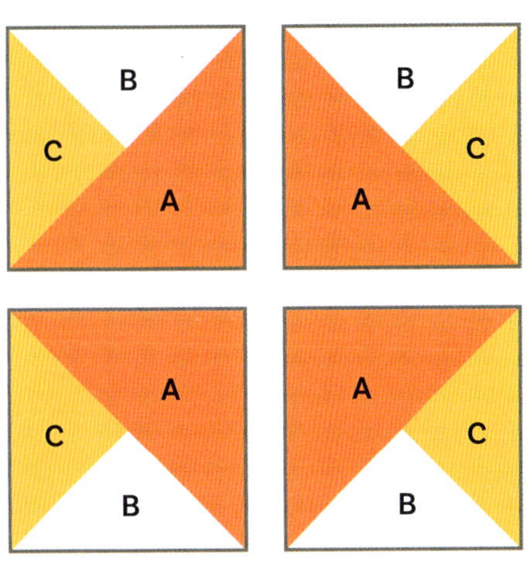

13 SPLIT QUARTER SQUARE TRIANGLE DIAMOND

Intricate and striking, this block positions Split Quarter Square Triangles to form a diamond shape at the center. It is perfect for adding complexity and visual interest to your crochet panels.

YOU WILL NEED

Crochet hook and yarn in three colors (see Yarn on page 9)
- Orange (A)
- Gray (B)
- Yellow (C)

Yarn needle

FINISHED MEASUREMENTS

5½ x 5½in (14 x 14cm)

Step 1: Make 4 x 3-round blocks as per Block 3 Split Quarter Square Triangle (see page 16), in A, B, & C.

Step 2: Weave in all ends (see page 124) and arrange the blocks in a 2 x 2 square with the A sections towards the center and the other colors positioned as shown in the diagram.

Step 3: Seam together with a yarn needle and A using the invisible seam technique (see page 125), first joining the vertical seams, then the horizontal seams. Weave in all ends and block as desired (see page 124).

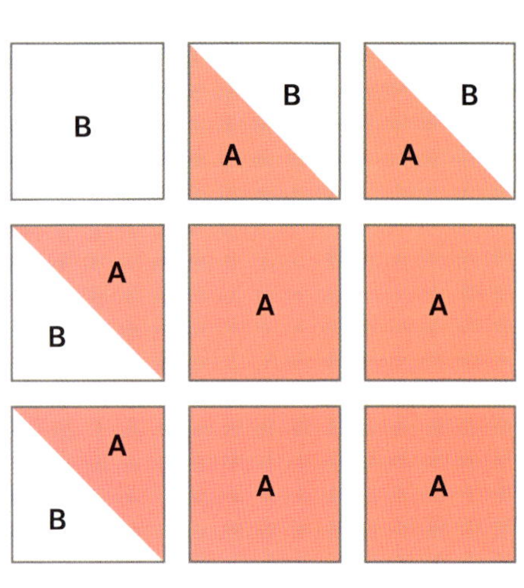

14 BEAR PAW

This bold and angular design uses small triangles to form "claws" reaching from a central square—it's often seen as a symbol of strength, trail-marking, and wilderness in traditional quilt designs.

YOU WILL NEED

Crochet hook and yarn in two colors (see Yarn on page 9)
- **Pink (A)**
- **Cream (B)**

Yarn needle

FINISHED MEASUREMENTS

8¼ x 8¼in (21 x 21cm)

Step 1: Make 5 x 4-round blocks as per Block 1 Plain Square (see page 12), with 4 in A and 1 in B. Make 4 x 4-round blocks as per Block 2 Half Square Triangle (see page 14), using A & B.

Step 2: Place the blocks in a 3 x 3 square in the orientation as shown in the diagram.

Step 3: Seam together with a yarn needle and A using the invisible seam technique (see page 125), first joining the vertical seams, then the horizontal seams. Weave in all ends and block as desired (see page 124).

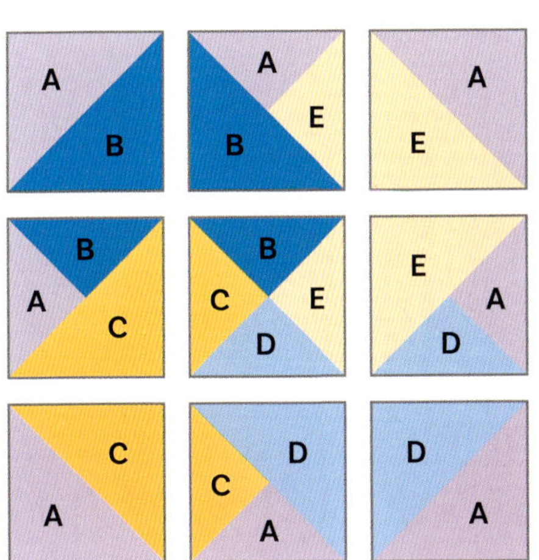

15 CARD TRICK

This block layers interlocking shapes to mimic overlapping playing cards and create a striking optical illusion. The secret to the design is all down to simple geometry and clever color placement.

YOU WILL NEED

Crochet hook and yarn in five colors (see Yarn on page 9)

- Lavender (A)
- Dark blue (B)
- Lemon yellow (C)
- Light blue (D)
- Pale yellow (E)

Yarn needle

FINISHED MEASUREMENTS

8¼ x 8¼in (21 x 21cm)

Step 1: Make 4 x 4-round blocks as per Block 2 Half Square Triangle (see page 14), 1 each using A & B, A & C, A & D, and A & E.

Make 4 x 4-round blocks as per Block 3 Split Quarter Square Triangle (see page 16), 1 each using B (main), A & E; C (main), A & B; D (main), A & C; E (main), A & D.

Make 1 x 4-round QST block as per Block 4 Quarter Square Triangle (see page 18), using B, C, D. & E.

Step 2: Place the blocks in a 3 x 3 square in the orientation as shown in the diagram.

Step 3: Seam together with a yarn needle and A using the invisible seam technique (see page 125), first joining the vertical seams, then the horizontal seams. Weave in all ends and block as desired (see page 124).

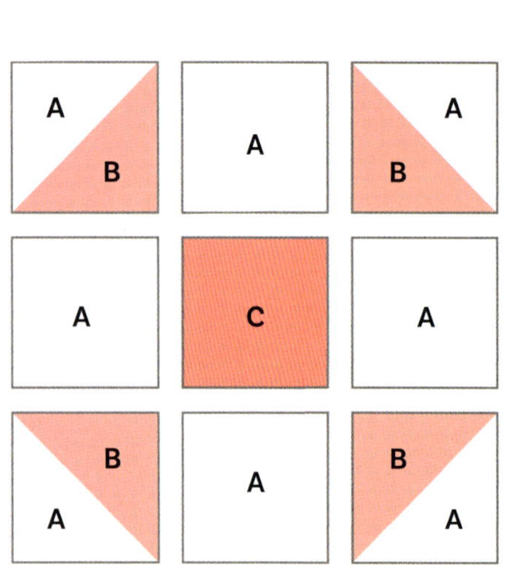

16 SHOO FLY

A traditional folk-style Nine Patch block, the Shoo Fly features diagonals at the corners and a central square, often symbolizing home and hearth in early American quilts.

YOU WILL NEED

Crochet hook and yarn in three colors (see Yarn on page 9)
- **Cream (A)**
- **Orange (B)**
- **Red (C)**

Yarn needle

FINISHED MEASUREMENTS

8½ x 8½in (22 x 22cm)

Step 1: Make 4 x 4-round blocks as per Block 2 Half Square Triangle (see page 14), using A & B. Make 5 x 4-round blocks as per Block 1 Plain Square (see page 12), with 4 in A and 1 in C.

Step 2: Place the blocks in a 3 x 3 square in the orientation as shown in the diagram.

Step 3: Seam together with a yarn needle and A using the invisible seam technique (see page 125), first joining the vertical seams, then the horizontal seams. Weave in all ends and block as desired (see page 124).

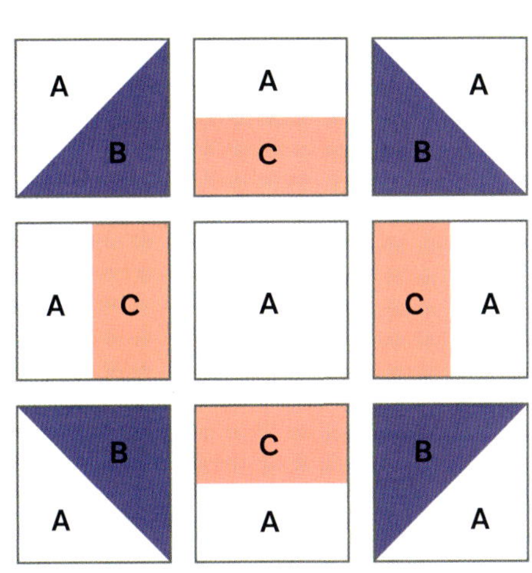

17 CHURN DASH

A traditional favorite, the Churn Dash uses a mix of HSTs and Rectangles to create a bold, framed shape. Its strong geometric lines make it a standout piece in any crochet quilt or afghan.

YOU WILL NEED

Crochet hook and yarn in three colors (see Yarn on page 9)
- Cream (A)
- Blue (B)
- Orange (C)

Yarn needle

FINISHED MEASUREMENTS

8½ x 8½in (22 x 22cm)

Step 1: Make 1 x 3-round block as per Block 1 Plain Square (see page 12) in A.
Make 4 x 3-round blocks as per Block 2 Half Square Triangle (see page 14), in A & B.
Make 4 x 3-round blocks as per Block 5 Rectangle Block (see page 20) in A & C.

Step 2: Weave in all ends (see page 124) and arrange the blocks into a 3 x 3 square as shown in the diagram.

Step 3: Seam together with a yarn needle and A using the invisible seam technique (see page 125), first joining the vertical seams, then the horizontal seams. Weave in all ends and block as desired (see page 124).

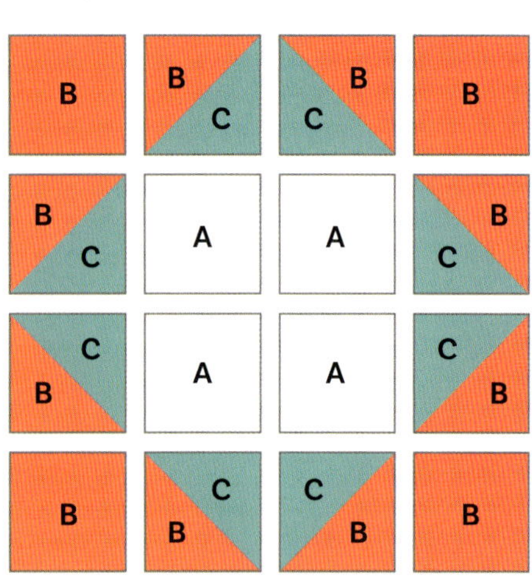

18 ECONOMY

Also known as the "Square-in-a-Square," the Economy Block features a centered square framed by two layers of triangles. This clean, balanced design is perfect for showcasing a focal color of yarn.

YOU WILL NEED

Crochet hook and yarn in three colors (see Yarn on page 9)
- **Cream (A)**
- **Orange (B)**
- **Mint green (C)**

Yarn needle

FINISHED MEASUREMENTS

11¼ x 11¼in (29 x 29cm)

Step 1: Make 8 x 3-round blocks as per Block 1 Plain Square (see page 12), 4 in A, 4 in B.
Make 8 x 3-round blocks as per Block 2 Half Square Triangle (see page 14), in B & C.

Step 2: Weave in all ends (see page 124) and arrange the blocks into a 4 x 4 square as shown in the diagram.

Step 3: Seam together with a yarn needle and A using the invisible seam technique (see page 125), first joining the vertical seams, then the horizontal seams. Weave in all ends and block as desired (see page 124).

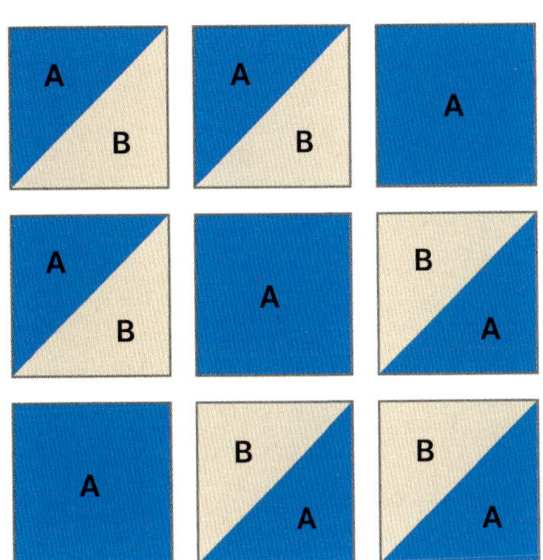

19 **MOSAIC**

Built entirely from Plain Squares and Half Square Triangles, this Mosaic Block creates a striking, tile-like design full of angles and contrast. A great way to explore color and symmetry in your crochet patchwork.

YOU WILL NEED

Crochet hook and yarn in two colors (see Yarn on page 9)
- **Blue (A)**
- **Beige (B)**

Yarn needle

FINISHED MEASUREMENTS

8¼ x 8¼in (21 x 21cm)

Step 1: Make 3 x 3-round blocks as per Block 1 Plain Square (see page 12), in A.
Make 6 x 3-round blocks as per Block 2 Half Square Triangle (see page 14), in A & B.

Step 2: Weave in all ends (see page 124) and arrange the blocks into a 3 x 3 square as shown in the diagram.

Step 3: Seam together with a yarn needle and A using the invisible seam technique (see page 125), first joining the vertical seams, then the horizontal seams. Weave in all ends and block as desired (see page 124).

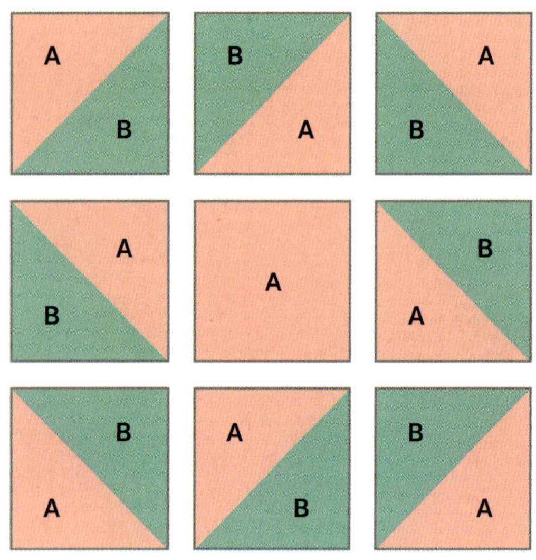

> **TIP**
> When working with blocks like this where lots of the elements are the same, it's easy to mix up the placement or orientation. Before seaming, lay out all the blocks in the correct order and direction, and double-check the layout to avoid unpicking later!

20 **RIBBON**

A striking design made from HSTs and a solid Plain Square, this creates the illusion of interwoven ribbons to form an internal four-point star. One of the simpler star designs, this is often seen in traditional quilting designs.

YOU WILL NEED

Crochet hook and yarn in two colors (see Yarn on page 9)
- Pink (A)
- Green (B)

Yarn needle

FINISHED MEASUREMENTS

8½ x 8½in (22 x 22cm)

Step 1: Make 8 x 4-round blocks as per Block 2 Half Square Triangle (see page 14), using A & B. Make 1 x 4-round block as per Block 1 Plain Square (see page 12), using A.

Step 2: Place the blocks in a 3 x 3 square as shown in the diagram.

Step 3: Seam together with a yarn needle and A using the invisible seam technique (see page 125), first joining the vertical seams, then the horizontal seams. Weave in all ends and block as desired (see page 124).

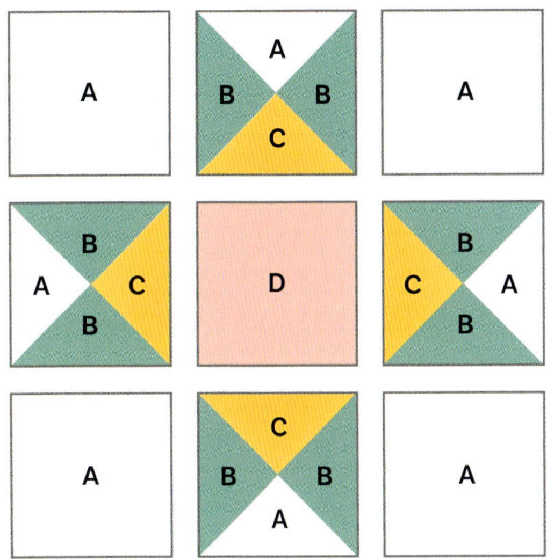

TIP

Use light, medium, and dark colored yarns to highlight the star's structure. Typically, the star points pop best in the darkest or boldest shade. Test your palette by arranging swatches—strong contrast helps the star stand out, while low contrast creates a muted look.

21 OHIO STAR

This classic block blends Plain Squares and HSTs to form a bold star within a square. With roots in American quilt history, the Ohio Star adds understated elegance and balance to your crochet compositions.

YOU WILL NEED

Crochet hook and yarn in four colors (see Yarn on page 9)
- Cream (A)
- Green (B)
- Yellow (C)
- Pink (D)

Yarn needle

FINISHED MEASUREMENTS

8¼ x 8¼in (21 x 21cm)

Step 1: Make 5 x 3-round blocks as per Block 1 Plain Square (see page 12), 4 in A and 1 in D.
Make 4 x 3-round blocks as per Block 4 Quarter Square Triangle (see page 18), in A, B (used twice) & C.

Step 2: Weave in all ends (see page 124) and arrange the blocks into a 3 x 3 square as shown in the diagram.

Step 3: Seam together with a yarn needle and A using the invisible seam technique (see page 125), first joining the vertical seams, then the horizontal seams. Weave in all ends and block as desired (see page 124).

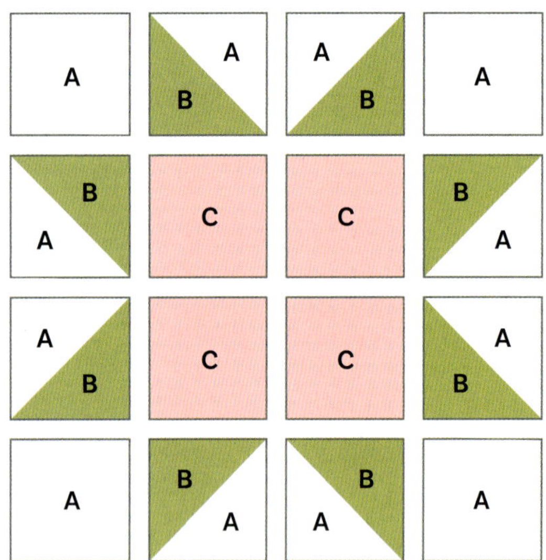

> **TIP**
> To help achieve invisible seams, pick a yarn that matches the lighter or background color in your blocks. Avoid dark yarns as they are more likely to show through. When in doubt, test on a scrap swatch to see how well the yarn blends in.

22 SAWTOOTH STAR

Featuring a bold central square framed by HST points, the Sawtooth Star is a crisp, high-impact block. Its clean lines and timeless appeal make it a favorite for both modern and traditional layouts.

YOU WILL NEED

Crochet hook and yarn in three colors (see Yarn on page 9)
- **Cream (A)**
- **Green (B)**
- **Pink (C)**

Yarn needle

FINISHED MEASUREMENTS

11 x 11in (28 x 28cm)

Step 1: Make 8 x 3-round blocks as per Block 1 Plain Square (see page 12), 4 in A and 4 in C. Make 8 x 3-round blocks as per Block 2 Half Square Triangle (see page 14) in A & B.

Step 2: Weave in all ends (see page 124) and arrange the blocks into a 4 x 4 square as shown in the diagram.

Step 3: Seam together with a yarn needle and A using the invisible seam technique (see page 125), first joining the vertical seams, then the horizontal seams. Weave in all ends and block as desired (see page 124).

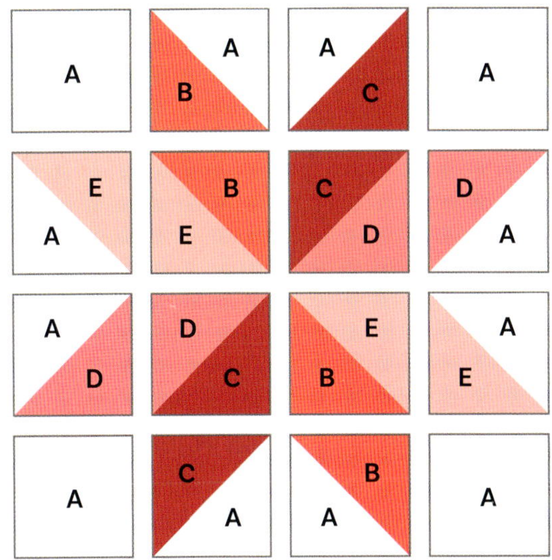

TIP

Using four shades of the same color adds depth and dimension. Choose yarns that range from light to dark within the same hue. This creates contrast while keeping the palette harmonious. Arrange your shades from lightest to darkest before starting, to help plan placement.

23 EIGHT-POINTED STAR

Vivid and vibrant, this eight-pointed star is worked in multiple shades or yarn colors to create a radiant, eye-catching centerpiece. Set against a plain background, the color play truly shines.

YOU WILL NEED

Crochet hook and yarn in five colors (see Yarn on page 9)

- Cream (A)
- Deep pink (B)
- Plum (C)
- Mid pink (D)
- Pale pink (E)

Yarn needle

FINISHED MEASUREMENTS

11½ x 11½in (29 x 29cm)

Step 1: Make 4 x 3-round blocks as per Block 1 Plain Square (see page 12) in A.
Make 12 x 3-round blocks as per Block 2 Half Square Triangle (see page 14), 2 in A & B, 2 in A & C, 2 in A & D, 2 in A & E, 2 in B & E, 2 in C & D.

Step 2: Weave in all ends (see page 124) and arrange the blocks into a 4 x 4 square as shown in the diagram.

Step 3: Seam together with a yarn needle and A using the invisible seam technique (see page 125), first joining the vertical seams, then the horizontal seams. Weave in all ends and block as desired (see page 124).

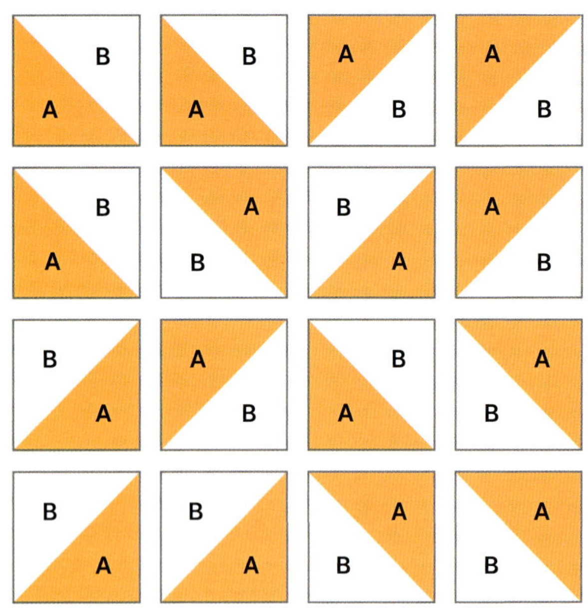

TIP

To make the star pop, choose two shades with strong contrast—a light and a dark from the same color family or complementary colors. The darker shade for the star points and the lighter shade for the background (and vice versa) will define the shape and create striking visual impact.

24 EIGHT-POINTED STAR—VARIATION

Using just two alternating colors for both the background and star, this version of the eight-pointed star delivers bold contrast and visual rhythm. The symmetry and simplicity highlight the graphic impact of the design.

YOU WILL NEED

Crochet hook and yarn in two colors (see Yarn on page 9)
- **Yellow (A)**
- **Cream (B)**

Yarn needle

FINISHED MEASUREMENTS

11 x 11in (28 x 28cm)

Step 1: Make 16 x 3-round blocks as per Block 2 Half Square Triangle (see page 14), in A & B.

Step 2: Weave in all ends (see page 124) and arrange the blocks into a 4 x 4 square as shown in the diagram.

Step 3: Seam together with a yarn needle and A using the invisible seam technique (see page 125), first joining the vertical seams, then the horizontal seams. Weave in all ends and block as desired (see page 124).

Chapter 3

COLORWORK BLOCKS

25 SNAIL TRAIL

Inspired by the foundation paper pieced block, this design creates a swirling pattern that makes a refreshing change to the angular nature of quilts with its striking spiral effect.

YOU WILL NEED

Crochet hook and yarn in four colors (see Yarn on page 9)
- Purple (A)
- Blue (B)
- Orange (C)
- Peach (D)

Yarn needle

FINISHED MEASUREMENTS

5 x 5in (13 x 13cm)

ABBREVIATIONS

ch - chain
dc - double crochet
hdc - half double crochet
RS - right side
sc - single crochet
sl st - slip stitch
sp - space
st(s) - stitch(es)
tr - treble
( ) - stitch sequences within round brackets are worked into the same stitch or space stated
[ ] - stitch sequences within square brackets are worked the number of times stated

Using A, make a magic ring.

Round 1 (RS): Ch1, (1sc, 1hdc, 1dc) into ring. Extend loop (so as not to lose st), remove hook and leave yarn. Using B, make a slip knot on hook, (1 standing sc, 1hdc, 1dc) into ring. Extend loop (so as not to lose st), remove hook and leave yarn. Using C, make a slip knot on hook, (1 standing sc, 1hdc, 1dc) into ring. Extend loop (so as not to lose st), remove hook and leave yarn. Using D, make slip knot on hook, (1 standing sc, 1hdc, 1dc) into ring. Extend loop (so as not to lose st), remove hook and leave yarn. Pull tail end to close magic ring.

Round 2 (RS): With hook pick up A loop, working in sts on previous round, 2hdc in first st (standing sc), 2dc in next st, 2dc in next st. With hook pick up B loop, working in sts on previous round, 2hdc in first st (standing sc), 2dc in next st, 2dc in next st. With hook pick up C loop, working in sts on previous round, 2hdc in first st (standing sc), 2dc in next st, 2dc in next st. With hook pick up D loop, working in sts on previous round, 2hdc in first st (standing sc), 2dc in next st, 2dc in next st.

Round 3 (RS): With hook pick up A loop, [1dc, 2dc in next st] 3 times (working over 6 sts from round below), with hook pick up B loop, [1dc, 2dc in next st] 3 times (working over 6 sts from round below), with hook pick up C loop [1dc, 2dc in next st] 3 times (working over 6 sts from round below), with hook pick up D loop, [1dc, 2dc in next st] 3 times (working over 6 sts from round below).

Round 4 (RS): With hook pick up A loop, [2dc, 2dc in next st] 3 times (working over 9 sts from round below), with hook pick up B loop, [2dc, 2dc in next st] 3 times (working over 9 sts from round below), with hook pick up C loop, [2dc, 2dc in next st] 3 times (working over 9 sts from round below), with hook pick up D loop, [2dc, 2dc in next st] 3 times (working over 9 sts from round below).

Round 5 (RS): With hook pick up A loop, 2tr, ch1, 2tr, 1dc, 1hdc, 1sc, 1 sl st. Fasten off A, cut yarn, draw tail through (do not pull up the sl st too tightly). With hook pick up B loop, 2tr, ch1, 2tr, 1dc, 1hdc, 1 sc, sl st. Fasten off B, cut yarn, draw tail through. With hook pick up C loop, 2tr, ch1, 2tr, 1dc, 1hdc, 1sc, sl st. Fasten off C, cut yarn, draw tail through. With hook pick up D loop, 2tr, ch1, 2tr, 1dc, 1hdc, 1 sc, sl st.

Fasten off D, cut yarn, draw tail through.

BORDER

Round 1 (RS): Attach A in any ch1-sp with 1 standing sc, (ch2, 1sc) in same sp, [1sc in each st to corner ch sp, (1sc, ch2, 1sc) in corner ch sp] 3 times, 1sc in each st to end, sl st to join.

Round 2 (RS): Ch1, 1hdc in same st, [(2hdc, ch2, 2hdc) in corner ch sp, 1hdc in each st to corner ch sp] 3 times, (2hdc, ch2, 2hdc) in corner ch sp, 1hdc in each st to end, sl st to join.

Fasten off.

26 LOG CABIN

A beloved traditional block, the Log Cabin is built around a central square, with strips added in a spiraling sequence. It symbolizes warmth and home—the center square is often seen in red because this represents a fire in the heart of a log cabin. This is perfect for creative color gradients or light–dark contrast.

YOU WILL NEED

Crochet hook and yarn in nine colors (see Yarn on page 9)
- Cream (A)
- Pale pink (B)
- Mid pink (C)
- Turquoise (D)
- Sky blue (E)
- Plum (F)
- Bright pink (G)
- Bright blue (H)
- Dark blue (I)

Yarn needle

FINISHED MEASUREMENTS

6 x 6in (15 x 15cm)

ABBREVIATIONS

beg - beginning
ch - chain
dc - double crochet
RS - right side
sl st - slip stitch
sp - space
st(s) - stitch(es)
WS - wrong side
( ) - stitch sequences within round brackets are worked into the same stitch or space stated
[ ] - stitch sequences within square brackets are worked the number of times stated

Using A, make a magic ring.
Round 1 (RS): Working into ring, ch3 (counts as 1dc throughout), 2dc, ch2, [3dc, ch2] 3 times, join with sl st to top of beg ch-3, turn. (*4 dc clusters, separated by ch-2 corners*)
Round 2 (WS): Sl st in corner sp, (ch3, 2dc, ch1) in corner sp, [(3dc, ch2, 3dc, ch1) in next corner sp] 3 times, (3dc, ch2) in last corner sp, join with sl st to top of beg ch-3. DO NOT turn work, stay with WS facing.
Fasten off A.
Row 3 (WS): Join in B in corner sp, working along one side only, ch3, 2dc in same sp, ch1, [(3dc, ch1) in next ch sp] twice, turn.
Row 4 (RS): Ch3, [(3dc, ch1) in next ch sp] twice, 1dc in top of ch-3 in row below.
Fasten off B.
Row 5 (WS): Turn and rotate work a quarter turn counterclockwise, join in C in top right corner sp worked in A, working along one side only, ch3, 2dc in same sp, ch1, [(3dc, ch1) in next ch sp] twice, 3dc, ch1 around side of dc worked in B, turn.
Row 6 (RS): Ch3, [(3dc, ch1) in next ch sp] 3 times, 1dc in top of ch-3 in row below.
Fasten off C.
Row 7 (WS): Turn and rotate work a quarter turn counterclockwise, join in D in top right corner sp worked in A, working along one side only, ch3, 2dc in same sp, ch1, [(3dc, ch1) in next ch sp] twice, 3dc, ch1 around side of dc worked in C, turn.
Row 8 (RS): Ch3, [(3dc, ch1) in next ch sp] 3 times, 1dc in top of ch-3 in row below.
Fasten off D.
Row 9 (WS): Turn and rotate work a quarter turn counterclockwise, join in E in top right corner sp worked in B, working along one side only, ch3, 2dc in same sp, ch1, [(3dc, ch1) in next ch sp] 3 times, 3dc, ch1 around side of dc worked in D, turn.
Row 10 (RS): Ch3, [(3dc, ch1) in next ch sp] 4 times, 1dc in top of ch-3 in row below.
Fasten off E.
Row 11 (WS): Turn and rotate work a quarter turn counterclockwise, join in F in top right corner sp worked in C, working along one side only, ch3, 2dc in same sp, ch1, [(3dc, ch1) in next ch sp] 3 times, 3dc, ch1 around side of dc worked in E, turn.
Row 12 (RS): Ch3, [(3dc, ch1) in next ch sp] 4 times, 1dc in top of ch-3 in row below.
Fasten off F.
Row 13 (WS): Turn and rotate work a quarter turn counterclockwise, join in G in top right corner sp worked in D, working along one side only, ch3, 2dc in same sp, ch1, [(3dc, ch1) in next ch sp] 4 times, 3dc, ch1 around side of dc worked in F, turn.
Row 14 (RS): Ch3, [(3dc, ch1) in next ch sp] 5 times, 1dc in top of ch-3 in row below.
Fasten off G.

Row 15 (WS): Turn and rotate work a quarter turn counterclockwise, join in H in top right corner sp worked in E, working along one side only, ch3, 2dc in same sp, ch1, [(3dc, ch1) in next ch sp] 4 times, 3dc, ch1 around side of dc worked in G, turn.
Row 16 (RS): Ch3, [(3dc, ch1) in next ch sp] 5 times, 1dc in top of ch-3 in row below.
Fasten off.

Row 17 (WS): Turn and rotate work a quarter turn counterclockwise, join in I in top right corner sp worked in F, working along one side only, ch3, 2dc in same sp, ch1, [(3dc, ch1) in next ch sp] 5 times, 3dc, ch1 around side of dc worked in H, turn.
Row 18 (RS): Ch3, [(3dc, ch1) in next ch sp] 6 times, 1dc in top of ch-3 in row below.
Fasten off.

27 MITERED LOG CABIN

With angled joins that meet at crisp corners, the Mitered Log Cabin is a variation motif and adds a tailored, architectural look to the classic log cabin style. It's ideal for showcasing clean lines and color framing in your crochet work.

YOU WILL NEED

Crochet hook and yarn in seven colors (see Yarn on page 9)
- Pale pink (A)
- Lilac (B)
- Purple (C)
- Pale blue (D)
- Bright blue (E)
- Plum (F)
- Bright pink (G)

Yarn needle

FINISHED MEASUREMENTS

5 x 5in (13 x 13cm)

ABBREVIATIONS

beg - beginning
ch - chain
dc - double crochet
RS - right side
sl st - slip stitch
sp - space
st(s) - stitch(es)
WS - wrong side
( ) - stitch sequences within round brackets are worked into the same stitch or space stated
[ ] - stitch sequences within square brackets are worked the number of times stated

Using A, make a magic ring.
Round 1 (RS): Working into ring, ch3 (counts as 1dc throughout), 2dc, ch2, [3dc, ch2] 3 times, join with sl st to top of beg ch-3, turn. *(4 dc clusters, separated by ch-2 corners)*
Round 2 (WS): Sl st in corner sp, (ch3, 2dc, ch1) in same corner sp, [(3dc, ch2, 3dc, ch1) in next corner sp] 3 times, (3dc, ch2) in last corner sp, join with sl st to top of beg ch-3. DO NOT turn work, stay with WS facing.
Fasten off A.
Row 3 (WS): Join in B in top right corner sp, working along one side only, ch3, 2dc in same sp, ch1, [(3dc, ch1) in next ch sp] twice, turn.
Row 4 (RS): Ch3, [(3dc, ch1) in next ch sp] twice, 1dc in top of ch-3 in row below.
Fasten off B.
Row 5 (WS): Turn and rotate work a quarter turn clockwise, join in C in top right corner sp worked in B, working along one side only, ch3, 2dc in same sp, ch1, [(3dc, ch1) in next ch sp] 3 times, turn.
Row 6 (RS): Ch3, [(3dc, ch1) in next ch sp] 3 times, 1dc in top of ch-3 in row below.
Fasten off C.
Row 7 (WS): Turn and rotate work a quarter turn counterclockwise, join in D in top right corner sp worked in B, working along one side only, ch3, 2dc in same sp, ch1, [(3dc, ch1) in next ch sp] twice, 3dc, ch1 around side of dc worked in C, turn.
Row 8 (RS): Ch3, [(3dc, ch1) in next ch sp] 3 times, 1dc in top of ch-3 in row below.
Fasten off D.
Row 9 (WS): Turn and rotate work a quarter turn clockwise, join in E in top right corner sp worked in D, working along one side only, ch3, 2dc in same sp, ch1, [(3dc, ch1) in next ch sp] 4 times, turn.
Row 10 (RS): Ch3, [(3dc, ch1) in next ch sp] 4 times, 1dc in top of ch-3 in row below.
Fasten off E.
Row 11 (WS): Turn and rotate work a quarter turn counterclockwise, join in F in top right corner sp worked in D, working along one side only, ch3, 2dc in same sp, ch1, [(3dc, ch1) in next ch sp] 3 times, 3dc, ch1 around side of dc worked in E, turn.
Row 12 (RS): Ch3, [(3dc, ch1) in next ch sp] 4 times, 1dc in top of ch-3 in row below.
Fasten off F.
Row 13 (WS): Turn and rotate work a quarter turn clockwise, join in G in top right corner sp worked in F, working along one side only, ch3, 2dc in same sp, ch1, [(3dc, ch1) in next ch sp] 5 times, turn.
Row 14 (RS): Ch3, [(3dc, ch1) in next ch sp] 5 times, 1dc in top of ch-3 in row below.
Fasten off G.

28 COURTHOUSE STEPS

This variation of the Log Cabin alternates strips evenly on opposite sides of the center square. The balanced layout creates a bold, stacked appearance and offers a structured, symmetrical feel to your project.

YOU WILL NEED

Crochet hook and yarn in five colors (see Yarn on page 9)
- Pale blue (A)
- Yellow (B)
- Turquoise (C)
- Orange (D)
- Green (E)

Yarn needle

FINISHED MEASUREMENTS

6 x 6in (15 x 15cm)

ABBREVIATIONS

beg - beginning
ch - chain
dc - double crochet
RS - right side
sl st - slip stitch
sp - space
st(s) - stitch(es)
WS - wrong side
( ) - stitch sequences within round brackets are worked into the same stitch or space stated
[ ] - stitch sequences within square brackets are worked the number of times stated

Using A, make a magic ring.
Round 1 (RS): Working into ring, ch3 (counts as 1dc throughout), 2dc, ch2, [3dc, ch2] 3 times more, join with sl st to top of beg ch-3, turn. (*4 dc clusters, separated by ch-2 corners*)
Round 2 (WS): Sl st in corner sp, (ch3, 2dc, ch1) in same corner sp, [(3dc, ch2, 3dc, ch1) in next corner sp] 3 times, (3dc, ch2) in last corner sp, join with sl st to top of beg ch-3.
Fasten off A.
Row 3 (RS): Turn work, join in B in corner sp, working along one side only, ch3, 2dc in same sp, ch1, [(3dc, ch1) in next ch sp] twice, turn.
Row 4 (WS): Ch3, [(3dc, ch1) in next ch sp] twice, 1dc in top of ch-3 in row below.
Fasten off B.
Row 5 (RS): Turn and rotate work a half turn, join in B in top right corner sp, working along one side only, ch3, 2dc in same sp, ch1, [(3dc, ch1) in next ch sp] twice, turn.
Row 6 (WS): Ch3, [(3dc, ch1) in next ch sp] twice, 1dc in top of ch-3 in row below.
Fasten off B.
Row 7 (RS): Turn and rotate work a quarter turn clockwise, join in C in top right corner sp worked in B, working along one side only, ch3, 2dc in same sp, ch1, [(3dc, ch1) in next ch sp] 3 times, 3dc, ch1 around side of dc worked in B, turn.
Row 8 (WS): Ch3, [(3dc, ch1) in next ch sp] 4 times, 1dc in top of ch-3 in row below.
Fasten off C.
Row 9 (RS): Turn and rotate work a half turn, join in C in top right corner sp worked in B, working along one side only, ch3, 2dc in same sp, ch1, [(3dc, ch1) in next ch sp] 3 times, 3dc, ch1 around side of dc worked in B, turn.
Row 10 (WS): Ch3, [(3dc, ch1) in next ch sp] 4 times, 1dc in top of ch-3 in row below.
Fasten off C.
Row 11 (RS): Turn and rotate work a quarter turn clockwise, join in D in top right corner sp worked in C, working along one side only, ch3, 2dc in same sp, ch1, [(3dc, ch1) in next ch sp] 3 times, 3dc, ch1 around side of dc worked in C, turn.
Row 12 (WS): Ch3, [(3dc, ch1) in next ch sp] 4 times, 1dc in top of ch-3 in row below.
Fasten off D.
Row 13 (RS): Turn and rotate work a half turn, join in D in top right corner sp worked in C, working along one side only, ch3, 2dc in same sp, ch1, [(3dc, ch1) in next ch sp] 3 times, 3dc, ch1 around side of dc worked in C, turn.
Row 14 (WS): Ch3, [(3dc, ch1) in next ch sp] 4 times, 1dc in top of ch-3 in row below.
Fasten off D.

Row 15 (RS): Turn and rotate work a quarter turn clockwise, join in E in top right corner sp worked in D, working along one side only, ch3, 2dc in same sp, ch1, [(3dc, ch1) in next ch sp] 5 times, 3dc, ch1 around side of dc worked in D, turn.
Row 16 (WS): Ch3, [(3dc, ch1) in next ch sp] 6 times, 1dc in top of ch-3 in row below.
Fasten off E.

Row 17 (RS): Turn and rotate work a half turn, join in E in top right corner sp worked in D, working along one side only, ch3, 2dc in same sp, ch1, [(3dc, ch1) in next ch sp] 5 times, 3dc, ch1 around side of dc worked in D, turn.
Row 18 (WS): Ch3, [(3dc, ch1) in next ch sp] 6 times, 1dc in top of ch-3 in row below.
Fasten off.

TIP

To increase the size of the square just increase in pattern as set in Row 4 to the desired size, then decrease as set.

29 STRING

This is a stash-busting favorite! Worked on the diagonal, the changing colors create a unique, striped-effect block. The yarn colors can be changed at the start or end of any row.

YOU WILL NEED

Crochet hook and yarn in eight colors (see Yarn on page 9)

Yarn needle

FINISHED MEASUREMENTS

4¾ x 4¾in (12 x 12cm)

ABBREVIATIONS

ch - chain
dc - double crochet
rep - repeat
RS - right side
sc - single crochet
sl st - slip stitch
sp - space
st(s) - stitch(es)
WS - wrong side
( ) - stitch sequences within round brackets are worked into the same stitch or space stated
[ ] - stitch sequences within square brackets are worked the number of times stated
*** - repeat sequence from * number of times stated**

Using first color, ch5.
Increasing rows.
Row 1 (RS): 4dc in last ch, turn.
Row 2 (WS): Ch4 (counts as 1dc and ch sp throughout), 3dc in sp between first 2 sts, miss 3 sts, 4dc in last ch sp, turn.
Row 3 (RS): Ch4, 3dc in sp between first 2 sts, miss 3 sts, 3dc in next sp, miss 3 sts, 4dc in last ch sp, turn.
Row 4 (WS): Ch4, 3dc in sp between first 2 sts, *miss 3 sts, 3dc in next sp; rep from * to last 4 sts, 3dc in last ch sp, turn.
Rows 5–8: As Row 4.

Decreasing rows.
Row 9 (RS): Ch3 (counts as 1dc throughout), miss 4 sts, 3dc in sp after 4th st, *miss 3 sts, 3dc in next sp; rep from * to last 4 sts, miss 3 sts, 1sc in last ch sp, turn.
Rows 10–12: As Row 9.
Row 13 (RS): Ch3, miss 4 sts, 3dc in sp after 4th st, [miss 3 sts, 3dc in next sp] twice, miss 3 sts, 1sc in last ch sp, turn.
Row 14 (WS): Ch3, miss 4 sts, 3dc in sp after 4th st, miss 3 sts, 3dc in next sp, miss 3 sts, 1sc in last ch sp, turn.
Row 15 (RS): Ch3, miss 4 sts, 3dc in next sp, 1sc in last ch sp.
Fasten off.

30 CIRCLE IN A SQUARE/ DRUNKARD'S PATH

This block is inspired by the Drunkard's Path, with the curved portions used here to create a circle in a square. A time-honored favorite, this has a visually striking design and has links to the traditional quilts of the Temperance movement.

YOU WILL NEED

Crochet hook and yarn in four colors (see Yarn on page 9)
- Light blue (A)
- Dark blue (B)
- Red (C)
- Pink (D)

Yarn needle

FINISHED MEASUREMENTS

4¾ x 4¾in (13 x 13cm)

ABBREVIATIONS

ch - chain
dc - double crochet
hdc - half double crochet
RS - right side
sc - single crochet
sl st - slip stitch
sp - space
st(s) - stitch(es)
tr - treble
WS - wrong side
( ) - stitch sequences within round brackets are worked into the same stitch or space stated
[ ] - stitch sequences within square brackets are worked the number of times stated

Using A, make a magic ring.

Round 1 (RS): Working into ring, ch3 (counts as 1dc throughout), 2dc in ring, change to B, 3dc in ring, change to a second ball of A, 3dc in ring, change to a second ball of B, 3dc in ring, sl st to join, turn.

Round 2 (WS): Ch3, 1dc in same st, 2dc in next 2 sts, change to A, 2dc in next 3 sts, change to B, 2dc in next 3 sts, change to A, 2dc in next 3 sts, sl st to join, turn.

Round 3 (RS): Ch3, 2dc in next st, [1dc in next st, 2dc in next st] twice, change to B, [1dc in next st, 2dc in next st] 3 times, change to A, [1dc in next st, 2dc in next st] 3 times, change to B, [1dc in next st, 2dc in next st] 3 times, sl st to join, turn.

Round 4 (WS): Ch3, 1dc in same st, [1dc in next 2 sts, 2dc in next st] twice, 1dc in next 2 sts, change to A, [2dc in next st, 1dc in next 2 sts] 3 times, change to B, [2dc in next st, 1dc in next 2 sts] 3 times, change to A, [2dc in next st, 1dc in next 2 sts] 3 times, sl st to join, turn.

Round 5 (RS): Change to C, ch1, 1sc in same st, 1sc in next st, 1hdc in next 2 sts, 1dc in next st, 3tr in next st, ch2, 3tr in next st, 1dc in next st, 1hdc in next 2 sts, 1sc in next 2 sts, change to D, 1sc in next 2 sts, 1hdc in next 2 sts, 1dc in next st, 3tr in next st, ch2, 3tr in next st, 1dc in next st, 1hdc in next 2 sts, 1sc in next 2 sts, change to second ball of C, 1sc in next 2 sts, 1hdc in next 2 sts, 1dc in next st, 3tr in next st, ch2, 3tr in next st, 1dc in next st, 1hdc in next 2 sts, 1sc in next 2 sts, change to second ball of D, 1sc in next 2 sts, 1hdc in next 2 sts, 1dc in next st, 3tr in next st, ch2, 3tr in next st, 1dc in next st, 1hdc in next 2 sts, 1sc in next 2 sts, sl st to join, turn.

Round 6 (WS): Ch3, 1dc in next 6 sts, 2dc in next st, 1dc in ch sp, 2dc in next st, 1dc in next 7 sts, change to C, 1dc in next 7 sts, 2dc in next st, 1dc in ch sp, 2dc in next st, 1dc in next 7 sts, change to D, 1dc in next 7 sts, 2dc in next st, 1dc in ch sp, 2dc in next st, 1dc in next 7 sts, change to C, 1dc in next 7 sts, 2dc in next st, 1dc in ch sp, 2dc in next st, 1dc in next 7 sts, sl st to join. Fasten off.

TIP

This version has been worked in quarters, assigning colors and shades to the quarters of the circle and square. It can be made with a single color for the circle and the square (see the dot block on page 102) or variations with multiple colors.

TIP

This block works well with carefully selected shades of a similar color, with a light, mid, and dark tone to create the 3-D effect.

31 ATTIC WINDOWS

Using clever angles and shading, this block creates a three-dimensional window frame effect. Rooted in the illusion of depth, this effect becomes especially striking when multiple blocks are combined.

YOU WILL NEED

Crochet hook and yarn in three colors (see Yarn on page 9)
- **Cream (A)**
- **Blue (B)**
- **Turquoise (C)**

Yarn needle

FINISHED MEASUREMENTS

4¾ x 4¾in (13 x 13cm)

ABBREVIATIONS

beg - beginning
ch - chain
dc - double crochet
RS - right side
sl st - slip stitch
sp - space
st(s) - stitch(es)
WS - wrong side
( ) - stitch sequences within round brackets are worked into the same stitch or space stated
[ ] - stitch sequences within square brackets are worked the number of times stated

Using A, make a magic ring.

Round 1 (RS): Ch3 (counts as 1dc throughout), 2dc, ch2, [3dc, ch2] 3 times, join with sl st to top of beg ch-3, turn. *(4 dc clusters, separated by ch-2 corners)*

Round 2 (WS): Sl st in corner sp, ch3, 1dc in same corner sp, 1dc in next 3 sts, [(2dc, ch2, 2dc) in next corner sp, 1dc in next 3 sts] 3 times, (2dc, ch2) in last corner sp, join with sl st to top of beg ch-3, turn.

Round 3 (RS): Sl st in corner sp, ch3, 1dc in same corner sp, 1dc in next 7 sts, [(2dc, ch2, 2dc) in next corner sp, 1dc in next 7 sts] 3 times, (2dc, ch2) in last corner sp, join with sl st to top of beg ch-3, turn.

Round 4 (WS): Sl st in corner sp, ch3, 1dc in same corner sp, 1dc in next 11 sts, [(2dc, ch2, 2dc) in next corner sp, 1dc in next 11 sts] 3 times, (2dc, ch2) in last corner sp, join with sl st to top of beg ch-3, turn.

Round 5 (RS): Change to B, sl st in corner sp, ch3, 1dc in next 15 sts, 2dc in next corner sp, change to C, ch2, 2dc in same sp, 1dc in next 15 sts, 1dc in ch sp, turn.

Round 6 (WS): Ch3, 1dc in next 17 sts, 2dc in next corner sp, change to B, ch2, 2dc in same sp, 1dc in next 18 sts, turn.

Round 7 (RS): Ch3, 1dc in next 19 sts, 2dc in next corner sp, change to C, ch2, 2dc in same sp, 1dc in next 20 sts. Fasten off.

32 ORANGE PEEL

Formed by curved petal shapes overlapping in a grid, this block is a vintage appliqué favorite—graceful and symmetrical, with echoes of floral and botanical motifs. Worked with small central shapes, it's a great stash-busting project.

YOU WILL NEED

Crochet hook and yarn in two colors (see Yarn on page 9)
  Lilac (A)
  Cream (B)

Yarn needle

FINISHED MEASUREMENTS

3¼ x 3¼in (8 x 8cm)

ABBREVIATIONS

ch - chain
cont - continu(e)ing
dc - double crochet
dtr - double treble
hdc - half double
RS - right side
sc - single crochet
sl st - slip stitch
sp - space
st(s) - stitch(es)
tr - treble
( ) - stitch sequences within round brackets are worked into the same stitch or space stated
[ ] - stitch sequences within square brackets are worked the number of times stated

Using A, ch14.

Round 1 (RS): Working in back bumps of ch, 1sc in second ch from hook, 1sc in next ch , 1hdc in next ch, 1dc in next ch, 1tr in next 5 sts, 1dc in next st, 1hdc in next st, 1sc in next st, 3sc in last st, rotate work and cont down other side of ch, 1sc in next st, 1hdc in next st, 1dc in next st, 1tr in next 5 sts, 1dc in next st, 1hdc in next st, 1sc in next st, 2sc in last st.
Fasten off.

Round 2 (RS): Join D at end of last round, 1 standing sc in first st, 1hdc in next 2 sts, 1dc in next 2 sts, 2tr in next st, (1dtr, ch2, 1dtr) in next st, 2tr in next st, 1dc in next 2 sts, 1hdc in next 2 sts, 1sc in next st, (1sc, ch2, 1sc) in next st, 1sc in next st, 1hdc in next 2 sts, 1dc in next 2 sts, 2tr in next st, (1dtr, ch2, 1dtr) in next st, 2tr in next st, 1dc in next 2 sts, 1hdc in next 2 sts, 1sc in next st, (1sc, ch2, 1sc) in next st, join with sl st to first st.

Round 3 (RS): Ch1, 1sc in same st, 1sc in next 7 sts, (1sc, ch2, 1sc) in ch sp, [1sc in next 9 sts, (1sc, ch2, 1sc) in ch sp] 3 times, 1sc in last st, join with sl st to first st.
Fasten off.

TIP

These blocks work well with a strong contrast between the center element and the outer block.

33 HEXI

This crochet granny hexagon is inspired by the classic patchwork quilt motif. Blending vintage charm with cozy texture, it's perfect for joining to create throws, bags, or garments—a modern application of a timeless design.

YOU WILL NEED

Crochet hook and yarn in five colors (see Yarn on page 9)
- **Cream (A)**
- **Yellow (B)**
- **Orange (C)**
- **Turquoise (D)**
- **Dark blue (E)**

Yarn needle

FINISHED MEASUREMENTS

5¼ x 5½in (13 x 14cm)

ABBREVIATIONS

beg - beginning
ch - chain
dc - double crochet
rep - repeat
RS - right side
sl st - slip stitch
sp - space
st(s) - stitch(es)
WS - wrong side
( ) - stitch sequences within round brackets are worked into the same stitch or space stated
[ ] - stitch sequences within square brackets are worked the number of times stated
*** - repeat sequence from * number of times stated**

Using A, make a magic ring.
Round 1 (RS): Working into ring, ch3 (counts as 1dc throughout), 2dc, ch2, [3dc, ch2] 5 times, join with sl st to top of beg ch-3, turn. *(6 dc clusters, separated by ch-2 corners)*
Fasten off A.
Round 2 (WS): Join in B, sl st in ch sp, (ch3, 2dc) in same ch sp, [(3dc, ch2, 3dc, ch1) in next ch sp] 5 times, (3dc, ch2) in last ch sp, join with sl st to top of beg ch-3, turn.
Fasten off B.
Round 3 (RS): Join in C, sl st in ch sp, (ch3, 1dc) in same ch sp, 3dc in next ch sp, [(2dc, ch2, 2dc) in next ch sp, 3dc in next ch sp] 5 times, (2dc, ch2) in last ch sp, join with sl st to top of beg ch-3, turn.
Fasten off C.
Round 4 (WS): Join in D, sl st in ch sp, (ch3, 1dc) in same ch sp, [3dc between dc clusters] twice, *(2dc, ch2, 2dc) in next ch sp, [3dc between dc clusters] twice; rep from * 4 times more, (2dc, ch2) in last ch sp, join with sl st to top of beg ch-3, turn.
Fasten off D.
Round 5 (RS): Join in E, sl st in ch sp, (ch3, 1dc) in same ch sp, [3dc between dc clusters] 3 times, *(2dc, ch2, 2dc) in next ch sp, [3dc between dc clusters] 3 times; rep from * 4 times more, (2dc, ch2) in last ch sp, join with sl st to top of beg ch-3.
Fasten off.

34 COLORWORK DIAMOND IN A SQUARE

This block features a striking diamond motif at the heart of a classic granny square. It adds a bold, graphic twist to a familiar structure—perfect for modern patchwork-style projects with a geometric flair. For a seamed version of this block, see page 28.

YOU WILL NEED

Crochet hook and yarn in two colors (see Yarn on page 9)
- Blue (A)
- Cream (B)

Yarn needle

FINISHED MEASUREMENTS

3¾ x 3¾in (9.5 x 9.5cm)

ABBREVIATIONS

beg - beginning
ch - chain
cont - continu(e)ing
dc - double crochet
rep - repeat
RS - right side
sl st - slip stitch
sp - space
st(s) - stitch(es)
( ) - stitch sequences within round brackets are worked into the same stitch or space stated
[ ] - stitch sequences within square brackets are worked the number of times stated
* - repeat sequence from * number of times stated

Using A, make a magic ring. All rounds are worked from the RS.

Round 1 (RS): Working into ring, ch3 (counts as 1dc throughout), 2dc, ch2, [3dc, ch2] 3 times, join with sl st to top of beg ch-3. (*4 dc clusters, separated by ch-2 corners*)

Round 2: Sl st in next 2 sts, sl st in next corner sp, (ch3, 2dc, ch2, 3dc, ch1) in corner sp, [(3dc, ch2, 3dc, ch1) in next corner sp] 3 times, join with sl st to top of beg ch-3.

Round 3: Sl st in next 2 sts, sl st in corner sp, join in B, do not cut A, (ch3, 2dc, ch2, 3dc, ch1) in corner sp, *pick up A, 3dc in next ch sp, ch1, pick up B, (3dc, ch2, 3dc, ch1) in corner sp; rep from * twice more, pick up A, 3dc in next ch sp, ch1, join with sl st to top of beg ch-3.

Round 4: Cont in B only, sl st in next 2 sts, sl st in corner sp, (ch3, 2dc, ch2, 3dc, ch1) in corner sp, *[(3dc, ch1) in next ch sp] twice, (3dc, ch2, 3dc, ch1) in corner sp; rep from * twice, [(3dc, ch1) in next ch sp] twice, join with sl st to top of beg ch-3.

Fasten off.

TIP

Note—do not cut the yarn between color changes, carry it behind the working yarn on the WS of the block.

35 LAYERED TRADITIONAL GRANNY DIAMOND

This motif layers classic granny-style stitches into a diamond shape, building texture and color in tiers. It merges the nostalgic feel of traditional grannies with dynamic, angular design—great for bold, eye-catching pieces.

YOU WILL NEED

Crochet hook and yarn in five colors (see Yarn on page 9)
- **Lilac (A)**
- **Yellow (B)**
- **Green (C)**
- **Pink (D)**
- **Blue (E)**

Yarn needle

FINISHED MEASUREMENTS

5¾ x 6¾in (15 x 17cm)

ABBREVIATIONS

beg - beginning
ch - chain
dc - double crochet
RS - right side
sl st - slip stitch
sp - space
st(s) - stitch(es)
tr - treble
WS - wrong side
( ) - stitch sequences within round brackets are worked into the same stitch or space stated
[ ] - stitch sequences within square brackets are worked the number of times stated

Using A, make a magic ring.

Round 1 (RS): Working into ring, ch3 (counts as 1dc throughout), 2dc, ch2, [3dc, ch2] 3 times, join wit sl st to top of beg ch-3, turn. *(4 dc clusters, separated by ch-2 corners)*

Fasten off A.

Round 2 (WS): Join in B, sl st in corner sp, ch4 (counts as 1tr throughout), 2tr in same sp, (3dc, ch2, 3dc) in next ch sp, (3tr, ch2, 3tr) in next ch sp, (3dc, ch2, 3dc) in next ch sp, (3tr, ch2) in last ch sp, join with sl st to top of beg ch-4, turn.

Fasten off B.

Round 3 (RS): Join in C, sl st in corner sp, (ch4, 2tr) in same ch sp, 3dc in next ch sp, (3dc, ch2, 3dc) in next ch sp, 3dc in next sp, (3tr, ch2, 3tr) in next ch sp, 3dc in next ch sp, (3dc, ch2, 3dc) in next ch sp, 3dc in next ch sp, (3tr, ch2) in last ch sp, join with sl st to top of beg ch-4, turn.

Fasten off C.

Round 4 (WS): Join in D, sl st in corner sp, (ch4, 2tr) in same ch sp, 3dc in next 2 ch sps, (3dc, ch2, 3dc) in next ch sp, 3dc in next 2 ch sps, (3tr, ch2, 3tr) in next ch sp, 3dc in next 2 ch sps, (3dc, ch2, 3dc) in next ch sp, 3dc in next 2 ch sps, (3tr, ch2) in last ch sp, join with sl st to top of beg ch-4, turn.

Fasten off D.

Round 5 (RS): Join in E, sl st in corner sp, (ch4, 2tr) in same ch sp, 3dc in next 3 ch sps, (3dc, ch2, 3dc) in next ch sp, 3dc in next 3 ch sps, (3tr, ch2, 3tr) in next ch sp, 3dc in next 3 ch sps, (3dc, ch2, 3dc) in nex ch sp, 3dc in next 3 ch sps, (3tr, ch2) in last ch sp, join with sl st to top of beg ch-4.

Fasten off.

36 LAYERED SOLID DIAMOND

Built with stacked, colorful rounds of solid stitches, this layered diamond creates a dense, textured shape with clean lines. Ideal for adding depth and structure, it's a fresh take on the traditional diamond motif.

YOU WILL NEED

Crochet hook and yarn in three colors (see Yarn on page 9)
- Turquoise (A)
- Purple (B)
- Blue (C)

Yarn needle

FINISHED MEASUREMENTS

5 x 7¼in (13 x 18.5cm)

ABBREVIATIONS

beg - beginning
ch - chain
dc - double crochet
RS - right side
sl st - slip stitch
sp - space
st(s) - stitch(es)
tr - treble
( ) - stitch sequences within round brackets are worked into the same stitch or space stated

Using A, make a magic ring. All rounds are worked from the RS.

Round 1 (RS): Working into ring, ch3 (counts as 1dc throughout), 1dc, 1tr, ch1, 1tr, 2dc, ch1, 2dc, 1tr, ch1, 1tr, 2dc, ch1, join with sl st to top of beg ch-3.

Round 2: Ch3, 1dc in next 2 sts, (2dc, 1tr, ch1, 1tr, 2dc) in next ch sp, 1dc in next 3 sts, (1dc, ch1, 1dc) in next ch sp, 1dc in next 3 sts, (2dc, 1tr, ch1, 1tr, 2dc) in next ch sp, 1dc in next 3 sts, (1dc, ch1, 1dc) in next ch sp, join with sl st to top of beg ch-3.

Round 3: Ch3, 1dc in next 5 sts, (2dc, 1tr, ch1, 1tr, 2dc) in next ch sp, 1dc in next 7 sts, (1dc, ch1, 1dc) in next ch sp, 1dc in next 7 sts, (2dc, 1tr, ch1, 1tr, 2dc) in next ch sp, 1dc in next 7 sts, (1dc, ch1, 1dc) in next ch sp, 1dc in last st, join with sl st to top of beg ch-3.

Fasten off A.

Round 4: Change to B, ch3, 1dc in next 8 sts, (2dc, 1tr, ch1, 1tr, 2dc) in next ch sp, 1dc in next 11 sts, (1dc, ch1, 1dc) in next ch sp, 1dc in next 11 sts, (2dc, 1tr, ch1, 1tr, 2dc) in next ch sp, 1dc in next 11 sts, (1dc, ch1, 1dc) in next ch sp, 1dc in last 2 sts, join with sl st to top of beg ch-3.

Fasten off B.

Round 5: Change to C, ch3, 1dc in next 11 sts, (2dc, 1tr, ch1, 1tr, 2dc) in next ch sp, 1dc in next 15 sts, (1dc, ch1, 1dc) in next ch sp, 1dc in next 15 sts, (2dc, 1tr, ch1, 1tr, 2dc) in next ch sp, 1dc in next 15 sts, (1dc, ch1, 1dc) in next ch sp, 1dc in last 3 sts, join with sl st to top of beg ch-3.

Fasten off.

Chapter 4

THE PROJECTS

TIP
When working with ultra fine cotton, gauge is key—keep your hands relaxed to avoid cramping and let the thread glide smoothly. Using a steel or fine-tipped hook can give you better control and cleaner stitches. Good lighting and a contrasting background will also help reduce eye strain and make the stitches easier to see.

BOOKMARK

SKILL LEVEL ● ● ○

Add a touch of charm to your reading with this delicate bookmark, crafted from ultrafine cotton for a refined finish. This pattern uses a traditional Split Quarter Square Triangle block (see page 16) worked with precision to create a lightweight yet vibrant design. Perfect for using up small amounts of thread, it's a quick and satisfying project that makes a lovely gift—or a personal treat for your next read.

YARN AND MATERIALS

Rico Essentials Crochet (100% mercerized cotton) crochet cotton weight, approx. 306yd (280m) per 1¾oz (50g) ball
1 ball each of:
Patina shade 024 (A)
Powder shade 014 (B)
Mustard shade 034 (C)

HOOK AND EQUIPMENT

US size 4/0 (1.75mm) steel crochet hook
Yarn needle

GAUGE

The first round of each granny square should measure approx. ½in (1.5cm) across. Gauge is not critical but can affect finished size and yarn amounts if not correct.

FINISHED MEASUREMENTS

5½ x 1½in (14 x 4cm)

ABBREVIATIONS

See page 127.

MAKING THE BOOKMARK

USING BLOCK 3 SPLIT QUARTER SQUARE TRIANGLE VERSION A: CLASSIC GRANNY SQUARE (SEE PAGE 16)

Make 5 x 2-round blocks in colors A (main), B & C.
Weave in ends and block as desired (see page 124).

MAKING UP AND FINISHING

Position the crochet blocks into a row of 5, using the photo as a guide.
Seam together with a yarn needle and B using invisible seam technique (see page 125).
Weave in ends.

BORDER

Round 1: With RS uppermost, join in C with a sl st in top left corner sp, ch3 (counts as 1dc throughout), 2dc, ch1, [3dc in next ch sp, ch1] 9 times, (3dc, ch2, 3dc, ch1) in corner sp, 3dc in next ch sp, ch1, (3dc, ch2, 3dc, ch1) in corner sp, [3dc in next ch sp, ch1] 9 times, (3dc, ch2, 3dc, ch1) in corner sp, 3dc in next ch sp, ch1, (3dc, ch2) in last corner sp, join with sl st to top of beg ch-3.
Fasten off C.
Round 2: Join in A, ch1, *1sc in each st to corner, (1sc, ch1, 1sc) in corner sp; rep from * to end, join with sl st to top of beg ch-1.
Fasten off and weave in all ends.

TASSEL

Cut six 4¾in (12cm) lengths of A and thread onto a yarn needle. Thread through the center stitch on the short side. Divide into three double strands and braid the length. Knot to secure leaving a short tassel. Trim the ends neatly to finish.

TIP

When sewing in ends on crochet projects using fine cotton, use a fine, sharp-tipped needle to avoid splitting the delicate threads. Weave the ends through several stitches in different directions to secure them neatly without bulk.

ATTIC WINDOWS TUB

SKILL LEVEL ● ● ●

Add a touch of three-dimensions to your space with this clever crochet tub, featuring an upper accent inspired by the Attic Windows quilt block (see page 64). Using angled stitches and color placement to create the illusion of depth, this pattern combines practical storage with the charm of traditional patchwork. It's ideal for showcasing tonal yarns or creating a 3-D effect with bold contrasts.

YARN AND MATERIALS

Lily Sugar n Cream (100% cotton) worsted (aran) weight, approx.119yd (109m) per 2½oz (70.9g) ball)
1 ball each of:
Tea Rose shade 00042 (A)
Tangerine shade 01699 (B)
Hot Orange shade 01628 (C)

HOOK AND EQUIPMENT

US size 7 (4.5mm) crochet hook
Yarn needle

GAUGE

First two rounds of each granny square should measure approx. 2in (5cm) across. Gauge is not critical but can affect finished size and yarn amounts if not correct.

FINISHED MEASUREMENTS

4¾in (12cm) tall x 5in (13cm) diameter

ABBREVIATIONS

See page 127.

MAKING THE TUB

USING BLOCK 31 ATTIC WINDOWS (SEE PAGE 64)

Make 6 x blocks in colors: A for 2 rounds of full square, then B & C for one side each in the next two half rounds.
Weave in ends and block as desired (see page 124).

MAKING UP AND FINISHING

Weave in all the ends and position the block into a strip following the same orientation for each square, using the photo as a guide.
Seam together with a yarn needle and A and using invisible seam technique (see page 125).
Fold the two shorter ends of the strip together and seam to make a loop.

UPPER BORDER

Join B in the first st of one of the squares along the upper edge with a sl st, ch1, *1sc in each of the 12 sts in this square, 1sc in last corner ch sp in this square; rep from * to end, join with a sl st to top of beg ch-1. *(78 sts)*
Fasten off and weave in ends.

LOWER BORDER

Round 1: Join in C on the lower edge in any st with a sl st, work 1sc in each st, 1sc in each corner ch sp of each square and 2sc in each row edge around, join with a sl st. *(78 sts in total, 13 sts per square)*
Round 2: Change to B, 1sc BLO each st.
Round 3: [2sc in first st, 1sc in next 38 sts] twice. *(80 sts)*

TIPS

For the lower border, I worked the single crochet stitches by taking the yarn under the hook rather than over the top as usual. This creates a squarer stitch that stacks up well, but you may find that the tub section will work up a bit smaller than the squares. To adjust this, you can size up the hook when working the tub section only.

When selecting the yarns for this project, choose high-contrast shades for the "window" and "shadow" sections to create a strong 3-D effect. Light, medium, and dark tones placed strategically will enhance the illusion of depth in the Attic Window block.

You could use this tub for storing anything from bathroom essentials to craft tools and yarn. It would also make a lovely plant-pot cover (see page 77).

Rounds 4–8: 1sc in each st.
Round 9: 1sc BLO in each st.
Decrease section:
Round 10: *1sc in next 8 sts, sc2tog; rep from * to end. *(72 sts)*
Round 11: *1sc in next 7 sts, sc2tog; rep from * to end. *(64 sts)*
Round 12: *1sc in next 6 sts, sc2tog; rep from * to end. *(56 sts)*
Round 13: *1sc in next 5 sts, sc2tog; rep from * to end. *(48 sts)*
Round 14: *1sc in next 4 sts, sc2tog; rep from * to end. *(40 sts)*
Round 15: *1sc in next 3 sts, sc2tog; rep from * to end. *(32 sts)*
Round 16: *1sc in next 2 sts, sc2tog; rep from * to end. *(24 sts)*
Round 17: *1sc in next st, sc2tog; rep from * to end. *(16 sts)*
Round 18: [Sc2tog] to end. *(8 sts)*
Round 19: [Sc2tog] to end. *(4 sts)*
Fasten off and weave in all ends.

SKILL LEVEL ● ○ ○

CHUNKY INTERSECTING DIAMONDS THROW

Wrap yourself in warmth and bold geometry with this eye-catching chunky throw. Featuring a patchwork motif of four intersecting diamonds, known as the Card Trick (see page 35), this design combines modern style with cozy comfort. Worked in thick yarn, it's a satisfying project that builds up quickly, making it ideal for adding texture and impact to your space.

YARN AND MATERIALS

Stylecraft Special XL Super Chunky (100% acrylic) super bulky (super chunky) weight, approx. 149yd (136m) per 7oz (200g) ball

- 4 balls of Parma Violet shade 1724 (A)
- 2 balls each of:
  - Denim shade 1302 (B)
  - Fuchsia Purple shade 1827 (C)
  - Cloud Blue shade 1019 (D)
  - Pale Rose shade 1080 (E)

HOOK AND EQUIPMENT

US size N/P-15 (11mm) crochet hook

Yarn needle

GAUGE

The first two rounds of each granny square should measure approx. 4¾in (12cm) across. Gauge is not critical but can affect finished size and yarn amounts if not correct.

FINISHED MEASUREMENTS

Approx. 54in (137cm) square

ABBREVIATIONS

See page 127.

MAKING THE THROW

USING BLOCK 2 HALF SQUARE TRIANGLE VERSION A: CLASSIC GRANNY SQUARE (SEE PAGE 14)

Make 4 x 8-round blocks, one in each of the following colors: A & B, A & C, A & D, A & E.

Weave in ends and block as desired (see page 124).

USING BLOCK 3 SPLIT QUARTER SQUARE TRIANGLE VERSION A: CLASSIC GRANNY SQUARE (SEE PAGE 16)

Make 4 x 8-round blocks, one in each of the following colors in the order given: B (main), C & A; C (main), D & A; D (main), E & A; E (main), B & A.

Weave in ends and block as desired.

USING BLOCK 4 QUARTER SQUARE TRIANGLE VERSION A: CLASSIC GRANNY SQUARE (SEE PAGE 18)

Make 1 x 8-round block, in the following colors in the order given: B, E, D, & C.

Weave in ends and block as desired.

MAKING UP AND FINISHING

Position the crochet blocks in a 3 x 3 square, using the diagram on page 35 as a guide.

Seam together with a yarn needle and A using invisible seam technique (see page 125), first joining the vertical seams, then the horizontal seams.
Weave in ends.

BORDER

Round 1 (RS): With RS uppermost join in A with a sl st in corner sp, ch3 (counts as 1dc throughout), 2dc, ch1, *[3dc in next ch sp, ch1] 7 times, 1dc in last ch sp of first square, 2dc in first ch sp of second square, [3dc in next ch sp, ch1] 7 times, 2dc in last ch sp of second square, 1dc in first ch sp of third square, [3dc in next ch sp, ch1] 7 times, (3dc, ch2, 3dc, ch1) in corner sp; rep from * twice more, [3dc in next ch sp, ch1] 7 times, 1dc in last ch sp of first square, 2dc in first ch sp of second square, [3dc in next ch sp, ch1] 7 times, 2dc in last ch sp of second square, 1dc in first ch sp of third square, [3dc in next ch sp, ch1] 7 times, (3dc, ch2) in last corner sp, join with sl st to top of beg ch-3, turn.
Round 2 (WS): Cont in A, sl st in corner sp, ch3, 2dc, ch1, *[3dc in next ch sp, ch1] 24 times, (3dc, ch2, 3dc, ch1) in corner sp; rep from * twice more, [3dc in next ch sp, ch1] 24 times, (3dc, ch2) in last corner sp, join with sl st to top of beg ch-3, turn.
Fasten off A.
Round 3 (RS): Change to B, sl st in corner sp, ch1 (does not count as a st), *(1sc, ch1, 1sc) in corner sp, 1sc in each dc and ch (not the ch sp) to next corner; rep from * to end join with sl st to top of beg ch-1.
Fasten off and weave in all ends.

TIPS

With chunky yarn, bulky ends can be tricky—so weave them into the thickest parts of your stitches, like at the base of a double or single crochet or between post stitches, to hide them securely. Use a blunt yarn needle and split the yarn plies as you go to anchor it without creating extra bulk. Always weave in at least 3-4in (7.5-10cm) and, if possible, change direction once to help lock the end in place.

Chunky yarn creates fast and cozy results, but the weight can build up quickly. To avoid hand and wrist strain, support your work as it grows—rest it on your lap or a table to reduce the pull on your hands. Use ergonomic hooks to ease tension, and consider working in shorter sessions with breaks to stay comfortable and keep your gauge consistent.

YARN AND MATERIALS

Caron Simply Soft (100% acrylic) worsted (aran) weight, approx. 315yd (288m) per 6oz (170g) ball

- 2 balls of Off White shade 9702 (A)
- 1 ball each of:
  - Robin's Egg shade 9780 (B)
  - Pumpkin shade 9765 (C)
  - Strawberry shade 0015 (D)
  - Blue Mint shade 9608 (E)
  - Blackberry shade 0005 (F)
  - Cool Green shade 9770 (G)
  - Lemonade shade 9776 (H)

3 pillow forms, 14in (35.5cm) square

HOOK AND EQUIPMENT

US size H-8 (5mm) crochet hook

Yarn needle

GAUGE

Each granny square should measure approx. 3in (8cm) across. Gauge is not critical but can affect finished size and yarn amounts if not correct.

FINISHED MEASUREMENTS

14in (35.5cm) square

ABBREVIATIONS

See page 127.

TRIO OF PILLOWS

SKILL LEVEL ● ○ ○

Bring cozy, crafted character to your space with this set of three crochet pillows, each built from sixteen mini granny squares. Drawing on the charm of traditional patchwork, these designs use color and placement to mimic classic quilt blocks—while keeping all the texture and warmth of crochet.

MAKING THE PILLOWS

BACK PANELS

Make 2 per pillow, one in each color
Granny Square Pillow 1: B & D
Economy Block Pillow 2: E & F
Pinwheel Pillow 3: G & H
Using first color, ch47.

Row 1: 1dc in 4th ch from hook (missed 3 ch count as a st), 1dc in each st to end, turn. (*45 sts*)

Rows 2–15: Ch3 (counts as 1dc throughout), miss first st, 1dc in each st to end, turn.

Row 16: Ch1, 1sc in each st to end.

Fasten off and weave in ends (see page 124).

TIP

These designs use solid granny squares to prevent too much of the pillow form from showing through to the right side. However, you can also choose to work the design using classic granny squares if you prefer.

GRANNY SQUARE PILLOW FRONT

USING BLOCK 1 PLAIN SQUARE VERSION B: SOLID GRANNY SQUARE (SEE PAGE 13)

Make 16 x 3-round blocks in the following colors:
8 in A, 3 in B, 2 in C, 3 in D.
Weave in ends and block as desired (see page 124).

MAKING UP AND FINISHING

Arrange the blocks in a 4 x 4 square using the photo as a guide.
Seam together with a yarn needle and A using invisible seam technique (see page 125), first joining the vertical seams, then the horizontal seams.

Place the front RS down and arrange the two Pillow 1 backing panels on top aligning the raw edges—there will be a slight overlap at the center. Pin into place.
Join in A, work 1sc in each st around to join front and back panels, joining through all layers, at corners work (1sc, ch1, 1sc) in corner sp.
Fasten off and weave in all ends.
Place the pillow form inside through the opening at the back.

ECONOMY BLOCK PILLOW FRONT

USING BLOCK 1 PLAIN SQUARE VERSION B: SOLID GRANNY SQUARE (SEE PAGE 13)

Make 8 x 3-round blocks in the following colors:
4 in A, 4 in E.
Weave in ends and block as desired.

USING BLOCK 2 HALF SQUARE TRIANGLE VERSION B: SOLID GRANNY SQUARE (SEE PAGE 15)

Make 8 x 3-round blocks in the following colors: E & F.
Weave in ends and block as desired.

TIP

When joining the elements with an invisible seam, take care to align the stitches on both sides for a smooth, even finish. Pull the stitches together at regular intervals to ensure the seam remains as neat and seamless as possible.

MAKING UP AND FINISHING

Arrange the blocks in a 4 x 4 square, using the diagram on page 38 as a guide.
Seam together with a yarn needle and A using invisible seam technique, first joining the vertical seams, then the horizontal seams.

Place the front RS down and arrange the two Pillow 2 backing panels on top aligning the raw edges—there will be a slight overlap at the center. Pin into place.
Join in A, work 1sc in each st around to join front and back panels, joining through all layers, at corners working (1sc, ch1, 1sc) in corner sp.
Fasten off and weave in all ends.
Place the pillow form inside through the opening at the back.

PINWHEEL PILLOW FRONT

USING BLOCK 2 HALF SQUARE TRIANGLE VERSION B: SOLID GRANNY SQUARE (SEE PAGE 15)

Make 16 x 3-round blocks in the following colors:
8 in A & G, 8 in A & H.
Weave in ends and block as desired.

MAKING UP AND FINISHING

Arrange the blocks in a 4 x 4 square using the diagram as a guide.

Seam together with a yarn needle and A using invisible seam technique, first joining the vertical seams, then the horizontal seams.

Place the front RS down and arrange the two Pillow 3 backing panels on top aligning the raw edges—there will be a slight overlap at the center. Pin into place.
Join in A, work 1sc in each st around to join front and back panels, joining through all layers, at corners working (1sc, ch1, 1sc) in corner sp.
Fasten off and weave in all ends.
Place the pillow form inside through the opening at the back.

YARN AND MATERIALS

Yarn And Colors Happy (25% wool, 25% acrylic, 50% polyamide) bulky (chunky) weight, approx. 148yd (136m) per 3½oz (100g) ball
- 2 balls of Cream shade 002 (A)
- 1 ball each of:
  - Denim shade 61 (B)
  - Glass shade 72 (C)

HOOK AND EQUIPMENT

US size J-10 (6mm) crochet hook

Yarn needle

GAUGE

Each granny square should measure approx. 3in (8cm) across. Gauge is not critical but can affect finished size and yarn amounts if not correct.

FINISHED MEASUREMENTS

66 x 6¾in (168 x 17cm)

ABBREVIATIONS

See page 127.

FLYING GEESE SCARF

SKILL LEVEL ● ○ ○

Wrap yourself in warmth and tradition with this crochet scarf inspired by the classic Flying Geese quilt block. Featuring bold, triangular motifs that echo the motion and balance of migrating geese, this design brings a touch of heritage craft to your handmade wardrobe. Perfect for showcasing color contrasts and geometric flair.

MAKING THE SCARF

USING BLOCK 2 HALF SQUARE TRIANGLE VERSION A: CLASSIC GRANNY SQUARE (SEE PAGE 14)

Make 40 x 3-round blocks in the following colors: 20 in A & B, 20 in A & C.

Weave in ends and block as desired (see page 124).

MAKING UP AND FINISHING

Position the blocks in pairs with either B or C at the bottom center to create the Geese element of the block (see page 29). Arrange the blocks in a 20 x 2 strip, with each pair of the same color block forming a triangle as shown.

Seam together with a yarn needle and A using invisible seam technique (see page 125). Fasten off and weave in all ends.

TIPS

When weaving in chunky yarn, split the plies and weave through stitches in multiple directions to reduce bulk and secure the tail.

For a nearly invisible join, seam through the back loops only. Align the pieces with the right sides facing up, and work through the back loop of each stitch on both pieces (see page 125). This will keep the seam flat and help hide the yarn. If the yarn feels too thick, try using a matching thinner yarn strand for a smoother finish.

This design can be customized by either working with more colors for the "Geese" in the center or by adding more geese blocks for a longer or wider scarf.

TIP

The Split Quarter Square blocks have a lot of dynamic shape and you can change the look of the wrist warmers by rotating the blocks. These blocks can be mirrored or positioned in the same orientation, as desired.

WRIST WARMERS

SKILL LEVEL ● ● ●

Keep your hands warm in style with these crochet wristies, featuring the dynamic shapes of Split Quarter Square Triangles. Drawing from traditional quilt blocks, this design plays with bold lines and contrasting colors to create a graphic, geometric look—perfect for adding a touch of heritage-inspired flair to your everyday accessories.

YARN AND MATERIALS

Sirdar Loveful DK (100% recycled acrylic) light worsted (DK) weight, approx. 344yd (315m) per 3½oz (100g) ball

1 ball each of:
Sky shade 109 (A)
Mist shade 101 (B)
Flame shade 104 (C)
Ocean shade 110 (D)

HOOK AND EQUIPMENT

US size G-6 (4mm) crochet hook

Yarn needle

GAUGE

First two rounds of each granny square should measure approx. 2in (5cm) across. Gauge is not critical but can affect finished size and yarn amounts if not correct.

FINISHED MEASUREMENTS

6 x 4in (15 x 10cm) measured flat

ABBREVIATIONS

See page 127.

MAKING THE WARMERS

USING BLOCK 3 SPLIT QUARTER SQUARE TRIANGLE VERSION A: CLASSIC GRANNY SQUARE (SEE PAGE 16)

Make 4 x 4-round blocks in colors: A (main), B & C. Weave in ends and block as desired (see page 124).

MAKING UP AND FINISHING

Place into two pairs until you are happy with the orientation.

Working on each pair of squares in turn, join down the side seam with D on one side using a flat slip stitch join. On the remaining side, join the two pieces with a flat slip st join with D, leaving 1in (2.5cm) gap in the middle—this will become the thumb hole.

TOP BAND

Round 1: On the upper edge, join in D, work 1sc in each st, ch sp and side seam join around, join with a sl st. *(36 sts)*

Rounds 2 and 3: Ch1, 1sc in each st, join with a sl st.
Fasten off.

THUMB SECTION

Round 1: Join in D at the top of the gap in the seam line, 1sc in 8 sts/ch sp along one side, rotate and work 1sc in 8 sts/ch sp along second side.

Round 2: Ch1, 1sc in each st, join with a sl st.
Fasten off.

CUFF

Join in D to any st with a sl st, ch7.

Row 1 (RS): 1sc in second ch from hook, 1sc in next 4 ch, sc2tog with last st in ch and next st on wrist edge. *(6 sts)*

Row 2 (WS): Sl st in next st on wrist edge, turn, sl st BLO in each st to end.

Row 3 (RS): Ch1, 1sc BLO to last st, sc2tog over last st in cuff and next st on wrist edge.

Row 4 (WS): Sl st in next st on wrist edge, turn, sl st BLO in each st to end.

Rep Rows 3 and 4 until length of cuff has been worked, ending on an even row.
Fasten off, leaving a long tail for seaming.
Repeat to make the second cuff in the same manner, ensuring that orientations are matching.
Use the yarn tail to seam the cuff with an invisible join seam. Fasten off and weave in all yarn ends.

TIP

The size of these hand warmers can be customized to larger or smaller hands—simply work more rounds on the central crochet block for a larger size and less for a smaller size. You will then need to adjust the number of stitches worked for the cuff sections.

STAR WALL HANGING

SKILL LEVEL ● ○ ○

This bold wall hanging puts a fresh spin on the classic star motif. Worked in super bright yarns for high impact, it combines traditional shapes with modern color for a piece that's both nostalgic and full of energy—perfect for making a statement on any wall.

YARN AND MATERIALS

Paintbox Yarns Cotton DK (100% mercerized cotton) light worsted (DK) weight, approx. 137yd (125m) per 1¾oz (50g) ball

1 ball each of:
Champagne White shade 403 (A)
Bubblegum Pink shade 451 (B)
Buttercup Yellow shade 423 (C)
Macaron Green shade 470 (D)

HOOK AND EQUIPMENT

US size G-6 (4mm) crochet hook

Yarn needle

12½in (32cm) dowel rod

GAUGE

Each granny square should measure approx. 3in (8cm) across. Gauge is not critical but can affect finished size and yarn amounts if not correct.

FINISHED MEASUREMENTS

10½in (27cm) square

ABBREVIATIONS

See page 127.

MAKING THE WALL HANGING

USING BLOCK 1 PLAIN SQUARE VERSION A: CLASSIC GRANNY SQUARE (SEE PAGE 12)

Make 5 x 4-round blocks in the following colors:
4 in A, 1 in D.
Weave in ends and block as desired (see page 124).

USING BLOCK 4 QUARTER SQUARE TRIANGLE VERSION A: CLASSIC GRANNY SQUARE (SEE PAGE 14)

Make 4 x 4-round blocks in the following colors:
A, B, C, B.
Weave in ends and block as desired.

MAKING UP AND FINISHING

Position the crochet blocks in a 3 x 3 square, using the diagram on page 43 as a guide.
Seam together with a yarn needle and A using invisible seam technique (see page 125), first joining the vertical seams, then the horizontal seams.

EDGING

Round 1: Join in B with a standing sc at one corner, [1sc in each st to corner sp, (1sc, 2ch, 1sc) in corner sp] 4 times, join with a sl st.
Round 2: Join in C with a standing sc at one corner, [1sc in each st to corner sp, (1sc, 2ch, 1sc) in corner sp] 4 times, join with a sl st.
Round 3: Join in B with a standing sc at one corner, [1sc in each st to corner sp, (1sc, 2ch, 1sc) in corner sp] 4 times, join with a sl st.
Fasten off and weave in all ends.

HANGING

Position the dowel along the upper edge. Join a length of B at the back of the work and sew through each st, looping the yarn around the dowel to secure into place.

Cut a length of twine or yarn for the hanging loop and knot to each end of the dowel to finish.

Fasten off and weave in all yarn ends.

TIPS

To ensure you get a really neat join at the point where four blocks meet, work the joining stitches in the corner of each square in a clockwise direction and draw up fully to align the points.

The QST block uses one of the yarn colors twice in the construction; you will find it easier to ball up a second small amount of B to ensure that you can work each color in turn, without having to cut and rejoin yarns.

SAMPLER THROW

SKILL LEVEL 

This sampler throw is a celebration of classic patchwork, reimagined in crochet. Featuring a variety of striking motifs—including hearts, Sawtooth and Eight-Pointed Stars, Churn Dash, and Pinwheels—it's a joyful mix of shape, color and texture. Worked in light worsted (DK) yarn, the throw brings the beauty of traditional quilt blocks into a cozy, modern crochet project. Whether you choose a curated palette or go full scrappy is up to you!

YARN AND MATERIALS

Stylecraft Special DK (100% acrylic) light worsted (DK) weight, approx. 322yd (295m) per 3½oz (100g) ball
- **4 balls of Cream shade 1005 (A)**
- **3 balls of Hint of Silver shade 1807 (B)**
- **1 ball each of:**
- **Sage shade 1725 (C)**
- **Aster shade 1003 (D)**
- **Cornish Blue shade 1841 (E)**
- **Spearmint shade 1842 (F)**
- **Shrimp shade 1132 (G)**
- **Apricot shade 1026 (H)**
- **Violet shade 1277 (I)**
- **Wisteria shade 1432 (J)**
- **Petrol shade 1708 (K)**
- **North Sea shade 2178 (L)**
- **Spice shade 1711 (M)**
- **Citron shade 1263 (N)**
- **Pomegranate shade 1083 (O)**
- **Pink Rhubarb shade 2175 (P)**
- **Fondant shade 1241 (Q)**
- **Powder Pink shade 1843 (R)**
- **Meadow shade 1065 (S)**
- **Dandelion shade 1856 (T)**
- **Black Shade 1002 (U)**

HOOK AND EQUIPMENT

US size G-6 (4mm) crochet hook

Yarn needle

GAUGE

Each granny square should measure approx. 2¾in (7cm) across. Gauge is not critical but can affect finished size and yarn amounts if not correct.

FINISHED MEASUREMENTS

Approx. 40 x 55in (102 x 140cm)

ABBREVIATIONS

See page 127.

EIGHT-POINTED STAR

(make 2)

USING BLOCK 2 HALF SQUARE TRIANGLE VERSION B: SOLID GRANNY SQUARE (SEE PAGE 15)

Make 24 x 3-round blocks in the following colors:
2 in each of C & B, D & A, E & B, F & A, C & A, D & B, E & A, F & B.
4 in each of E & C, F & D.
Assemble following the instructions in Eight-Pointed Star Block on page 47.
Weave in ends and block as desired (see page 124).

SAWTOOTH STAR

(make 2)

USING BLOCK 1 PLAIN SQUARE VERSION B: SOLID GRANNY SQUARE (SEE PAGE 13)

Make 8 x 3-round blocks in H.

USING BLOCK 2 HALF SQUARE TRIANGLE VERSION B: SOLID GRANNY SQUARE (SEE PAGE 15)

Make 16 x 3-round blocks in the following colors:
8 in each of G & B, G & A.

Assemble following the instructions in Sawtooth Star Block on page 44.
Weave in ends and block as desired.

FLYING GEESE BANNER

(make 2)

USING BLOCK 2 HALF SQUARE TRIANGLE VERSION B: SOLID GRANNY SQUARE (SEE PAGE 15)

Make 24 x 3-round blocks in the following colors:
8 in each of I & A, I & B.
4 in each of J & A, J & B.
Assemble following the instructions in Flying Geese on page 29.
Weave in ends and block as desired.

DOT BLOCK

USING BLOCK 30 CIRCLE IN A SQUARE/DRUNKARD'S PATH PATTERN (SEE PAGE 62)

Make 3 x 3-round blocks in A & K following this modified pattern:
Using K, make a magic ring.
Round 1: Ch3 (counts as 1dc throughout), 11dc into ring, sl st to top of beg 3-ch. (*12 sts*)
Round 2: 2sc in each st, sl st to join. (*24 sts*)
Round 3: Change to A, *1sc in next 3 sts, 1hdc in next st, (1dc, 1tr, ch2, 1tr, 1dc) in next st for corner, 1hdc in next st; rep from * 3 times more, 1hdc in next st, sl st to join.
Round 4: Ch1, 1sc in first st, [1sc in next 8 sts, (1sc, ch1, 1sc) in corner st] 3 times, 1sc in last 9 sts, (1sc, ch1) in first corner st to complete corner, join with a sl st.
Fasten off.
Weave in all ends and block as desired.

HEART

USING BLOCK 2 HALF SQUARE TRIANGLE VERSION B: SOLID GRANNY SQUARE (SEE PAGE 15)

Make 14 x 3-round blocks in the following colors:
1 in each of B & O, A & P, B & Q, Q & R, O & Q, R & P, P & Q
2 in each of B & P, O & R.
3 in A & O.
Weave in all ends and arrange the blocks in a 4 x 4 square as shown in the photo.

Seam together with a yarn needle and A using the invisible seam technique (see page 125), first joining the vertical seams, then the horizontal seams.
Weave in ends and block as desired.

PINWHEEL BLOCKS

(make 4)

USING BLOCK 2 HALF SQUARE TRIANGLE VERSION B: SOLID GRANNY SQUARE (SEE PAGE 15)

Make 16 x 3-round blocks in the following colors:
4 in each of M & A, M & B.
2 in each of N & A, N & B, L & A, L & B.
Assemble following the instructions in Pinwheel on page 31.
Weave in ends and block as desired.

CHURN DASH

(make 2)

USING BLOCK 1 PLAIN SQUARE VERSION B: SOLID GRANNY SQUARE (SEE PAGE 13)

Make 2 x 3-round blocks in the following colors: 1 in B, 1 in A.

USING BLOCK 2 HALF SQUARE TRIANGLE VERSION B: SOLID GRANNY SQUARE (SEE PAGE 15)

Make 8 x 3-round blocks in the following colors: 4 in each of F & A, F & B.

USING BLOCK 5 RECTANGLE BLOCK: SOLID GRANNY SQUARE (SEE PAGE 20)

Make 8 x 3-round blocks in the following colors: 4 each in S & A, S & B.

Assemble following the instructions in Churn Dash on page 37.

Weave in ends and block as desired.

TIPS

This throw is made with lots of squares and using lots of different colors. Try to weave in the ends of each square as you complete it so that you aren't faced with hundreds of ends to weave in when you complete the throw.

Since this is a really large project you may prefer to seam each of the individual blocks in turn and then seam to create the whole throw. Alternatively, if you have space to lay out the whole design, you can work by seaming the throw in horizontal rows then working the vertical seams.

EIGHT-POINTED STAR VARIATION

USING BLOCK 2 HALF SQUARE TRIANGLE VERSION B: SOLID GRANNY SQUARE (SEE PAGE 15)

Make 16 x 3-round blocks in the following colors: A & T.

Assemble following the instructions in Eight-Pointed Star—Variation on page 48.

Weave in ends and block as desired.

BACKGROUND BLOCKS

(make 127)

USING THE BLOCK 1 PLAIN SQUARE VERSION B: SOLID GRANNY SQUARE (SEE PAGE 13)

Make 127 x 3-round blocks in the following colors: 62 in A, 65 in B.

Weave in all ends and block as desired.

MAKING UP AND FINISHING

This throw is made up of 19 rows of 14 blocks (266 blocks). Using the diagram as a guide, position the blocks into rows, or arrange into motifs for seaming.

Seam together with a yarn needle and A using invisible seam technique, first joining the vertical seams, then the horizontal seams.

BORDER

Join in U with a standing sc on one short side with RS uppermost.

Round 1: *1sc in each st to corner, (1sc, 2ch, 1sc) in corner; rep from * to end, join with a sl st.

Fasten off U, join in A with a standing sc.

Round 2: *1sc in each st to corner, (1sc, 2ch, 1sc) in corner; rep from * to end, join with a sl st.

Fasten off A, join in U with a standing sc.

Round 3: *1sc in each st to corner, (1sc, 2ch, 1sc) in corner; rep from * to end, join with a sl st.

Fasten off and weave in all ends.

ORANGE PEEL BAG

SKILL LEVEL ● ● ●

This small but roomy bag is made using the Orange Peel block, inspired by the classic quilting motif. The curved shape is recreated with layered stitches and color contrast, giving the bag a bold, graphic look. Although compact, clever seaming adds depth and structure, making it surprisingly spacious. Worked in light worsted (DK) yarn, it's perfect for experimenting with color and value. A quick, satisfying project blending patchwork style and practical use.

YARN AND MATERIALS

Sirdar Happy Cotton DK (100% cotton) light worsted (DK) weight, approx. 47yd (43m) per ¾oz (20g) ball

- 4 balls of Fizz shade 779 (A)
- 1 ball each of:
  - Jammy shade 755 (B)
  - Currant Bun shade 756 (C)
  - Quack shade 788 (D)
  - Seaside shade 784 (E)
  - Giggle shade 795 (F)
  - Juicy shade 792 (G)
  - Princess shade 798 (H)

HOOK AND EQUIPMENT

US size G-6 (4mm) crochet hook

Yarn needle

GAUGE

Each square should measure approx. 3in (7.5cm) across. Gauge is not critical but can affect finished size and yarn amounts if not correct.

FINISHED MEASUREMENTS

14in (35.5cm) square

8¾in high x 8¾in wide laid flat without straps (22 x 22cm)

ABBREVIATIONS

See page 127.

TIP

Before you start seaming, use locking stitch markers or even quilter's clips to align the edges and keep the pieces steady. Mark key points like corners or halfway marks to ensure an even join. This helps prevent shifting as you seam and makes it easier to keep your slip stitches consistent—especially when working through the back loops only.

MAKING THE BAG

USING BLOCK 32 ORANGE PEEL BLOCK (SEE PAGE 66)

Make 13 x 3-round blocks using A as the outer color and working the center section in the following colors: 2 each of B, C, D, E, F & G, 1 of H.

Weave in ends and block as desired (see page 124).

MAKING UP AND FINISHING

Position the crochet blocks into rows, placed on the diagonal, following the diagram as a guide.

Seam together with the crochet hook and A using flat slip stitch seam technique, first joining the panels along the diagonal seams to create a flat panel.

Fold the bag in half through the H center block—this will form the base. Fold the two sides through the two D center blocks.

Seam the bag along the F and G center blocks on each side to make the lower side seams.

EDGING

Join A and work 1sc in each st around upper edge, at each of four top points working (1sc, 1ch, 1sc), join with a sl st.
Fasten off.

STRAPS

(make 2)
Join A along one pointed tip, 3sc, *ch1, turn, 1sc in each st; rep from * until work measures 13in (33cm).
Seam each end of strap at top on same side of bag.
Fasten off and weave in all ends.

TIP

When crocheting the handles for the bag, consider working each in turn and seaming when complete to ensure that the handles are the same length.

SKILL LEVEL 

PATCHWORK KIMONO-STYLE CARDIGAN

This simple kimono-style cardigan is made from bold Split Quarter Square Triangle and Half Square Triangle motifs. With minimal shaping and a relaxed fit, it's an easy, modular project suitable for all levels. Worked in worsted (aran) weight yarn, it's perfect for showcasing color and contrast.

YARN AND MATERIALS

Caron Simply Soft (100% acrylic) worsted (aran) weight, approx. 315yd (288m) per 6oz (170g) ball
- 3 balls of Off White shade 9702 (A)
- 1 ball each of:
  - Watermelon shade 9604 (B)
  - Blue Mint shade 9608 (C)
  - Lemonade shade 9776 (D)
  - Neon Orange shade 9774 (E)

HOOK AND EQUIPMENT

US size H-8 (5mm) crochet hook

Yarn needle

GAUGE

Each granny square should measure approx. 4in (10cm) across. Gauge is not critical but can affect finished size and yarn amounts if not correct.

FINISHED MEASUREMENTS

24in (61cm) width across back; 25½in (65cm) length; 17¼in (44cm) sleeve length (see Tip for adjusting size)

ABBREVIATIONS

See page 127.

MAKING THE CARDIGAN

USING BLOCK 1 PLAIN SQUARE VERSION A: CLASSIC GRANNY SQUARE (SEE PAGE 12)

Make 20 x 4-round blocks in the following colors:
16 in A, 4 in B.
Weave in ends and block as desired (see page 124).

USING BLOCK 2 HALF SQUARE TRIANGLE VERSION A: CLASSIC GRANNY SQUARE (SEE PAGE 14)

Make 64 x 4-round blocks in the following colors:
16 in A & B, 12 in A & C, 24 in A & D, 12 in A & E.
Weave in ends and block as desired.

USING BLOCK 3 SPLIT QUARTER SQUARE TRIANGLE VERSION A: CLASSIC GRANNY SQUARE (SEE PAGE 16)

Make 8 x 4-round blocks in the following colors:
C (main), E & A in that order.
Weave in ends and block as desired.

MAKING UP AND FINISHING

Position the crochet blocks into rows following the diagram as a guide.
Seam together with a yarn needle and A using invisible seam technique (see page 125), first joining the vertical seams, then the horizontal seams.
Weave in ends.
Once the piece is seamed flat, fold in half with WS facing and aligning lower hems at front and back.
Seam the underarm and side seam in one continuous seam. Repeat for the other side.

TIP

This cardigan can be made to a custom fit. Here the squares are made to four rounds and measure 4in (10cm) square. The back measurement (taken along the back from side seam to side seam) measures 24in (61cm). To increase the size work more rounds on the granny square as a swatch. From that calculate the desired size that you require to suit your preferred back measurement. Remember you will need to increase the yarn amounts to accommodate larger sizes.

CUFF EDGING

Join B along the lower edge of one cuff and work 1sc in each st and joined seam around, join with a sl st.
Work one more round, working 1sc in each st around, join with a sl st.
Fasten off.
Repeat for second sleeve.

EDGING

Join B at lower left front of cardigan opening, and work 1sc in each st around lower hem, up front edge, around neck and down front to end at lower hem, join with a sl st.
Rep for one more round.
Fasten off and weave in all ends.

TECHNIQUES

This section guides you through all the crochet and finishing techniques that you will need to make the blocks and projects in this book.

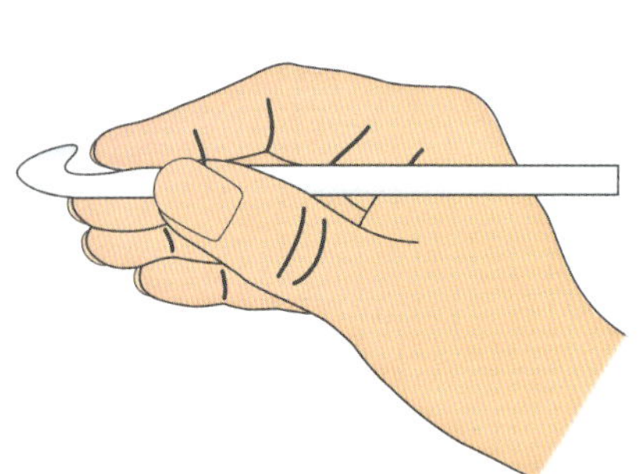

Holding the hook

Pick up your hook as though you are picking up a pen or pencil. Keeping the hook held loosely between your fingers and thumb, turn your hand so that the palm is facing up and the hook is balanced in your hand and resting in the space between your index finger and your thumb.

You can also hold the hook like a knife—this may be easier if you are working with a large hook or with bulky (chunky) yarn. Choose the method that you find most comfortable.

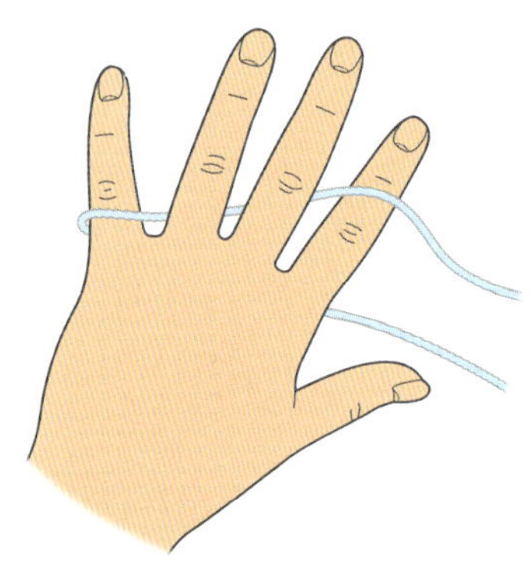

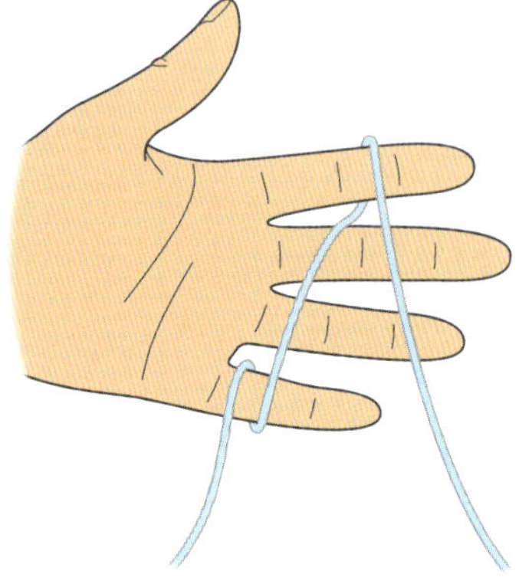

Holding the yarn

1 Pick up the yarn with your little finger in the opposite hand to your hook, with your palm facing upward and with the short end in front. Turn your hand to face downward, with the yarn on top of your index finger and under the other two fingers and wrapped right around the little finger, as shown above.

2 Turn your hand to face you, ready to hold the work in your middle finger and thumb. Keeping your index finger only at a slight curve, hold the work or the slip knot using the same hand, between your middle finger and your thumb and just below the crochet hook and loop/s on the hook.

Holding the hook and yarn while crocheting

Keep your index finger, with the yarn draped over it, at a slight curve, and hold your work (or the slip knot) using the same hand, between your middle finger and your thumb and just below the crochet hook and loop/s on the hook.

As you draw the loop through the hook release the yarn on the index finger to allow the loop to stay loose on the hook. If you tense your index finger, the yarn will become too tight and pull the loop on the hook too tight for you to draw the yarn through.

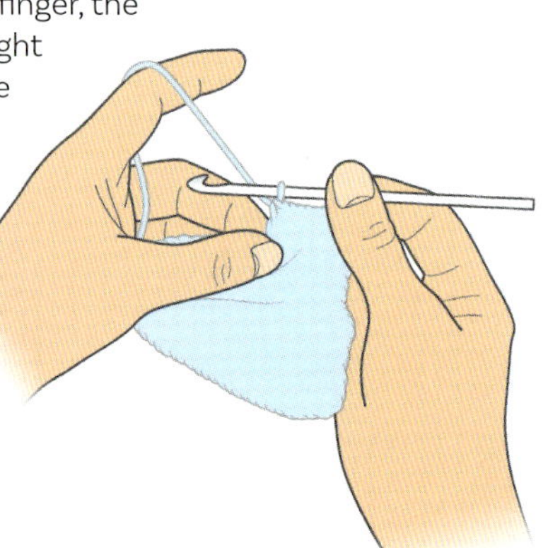

Holding the hook and yarn for left-handers

Some left-handers learn to crochet like right-handers, but others learn with everything reversed—with the hook in the left hand and the yarn in the right.

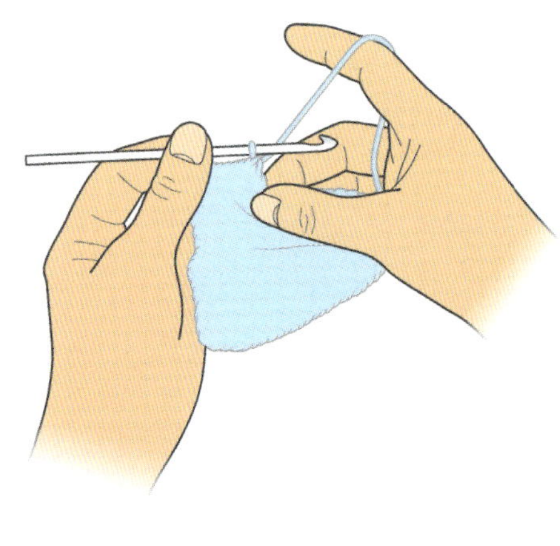

Making a slip knot

The simplest way is to make a circle with the yarn, so that the loop is facing downward.

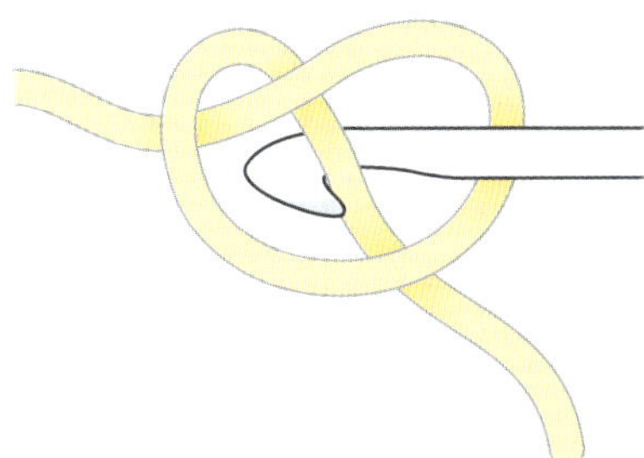

1 In one hand hold the circle at the top where the yarn crosses, and let the tail drop down at the back so that it falls across the center of the loop. With your free hand or the tip of a crochet hook, pull a loop through the circle.

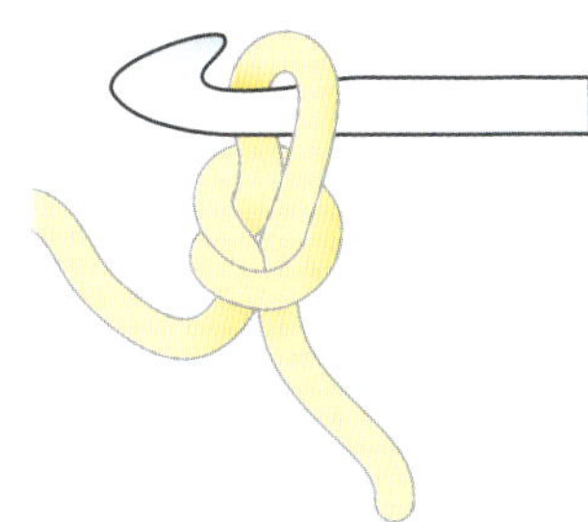

2 Put the hook into the loop and pull gently so that it forms a loose loop on the hook.

Yarn over hook (yoh)

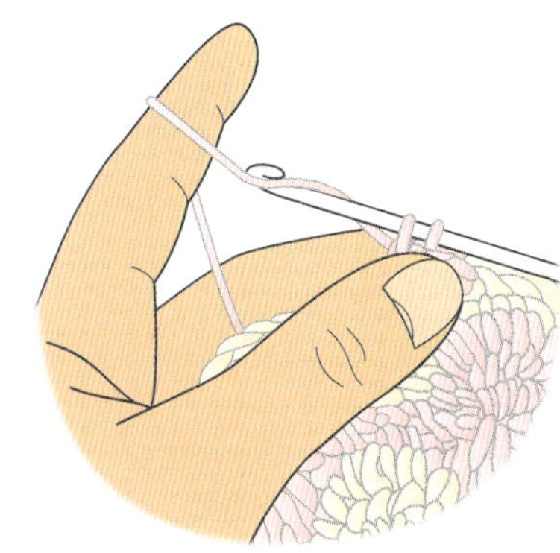

To create a stitch, catch the yarn from behind with the hook pointing upward. As you gently pull the yarn through the loop on the hook, turn the hook so it faces downward and slide the yarn through the loop. The loop on the hook should be kept loose enough for the hook to slide through easily.

Chain (ch)

1 Using the hook, wrap the yarn over the hook ready to pull it through the loop on the hook.

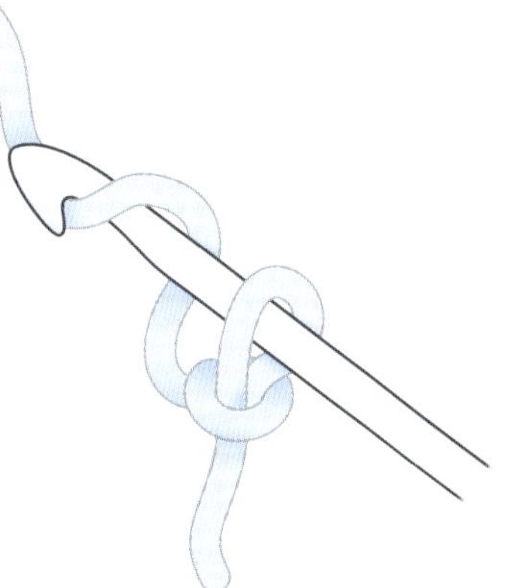

2 Pull through, creating a new loop on the hook. Continue in this way to create a chain of the required length.

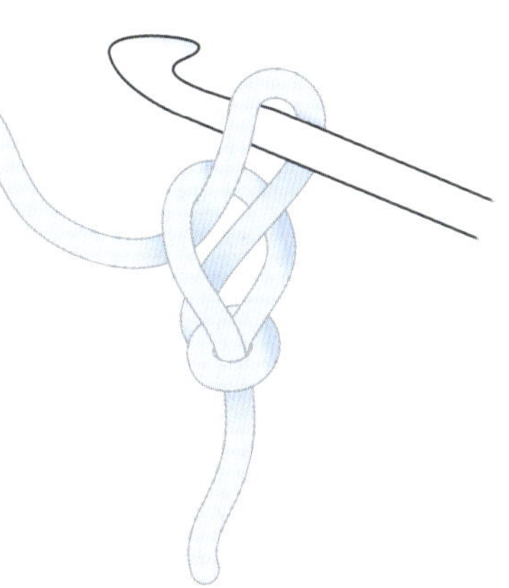

Working into a foundation chain

Working into the front of the foundation chain

The front of the chain (the right side) is the smooth side: each chain makes a little "V," as shown here. To make the first stitch into your foundation chain, using the point of the tip of the hook and with the hook tilted slightly sideways, insert the hook into the middle of the chain, picking up the loop at the top of the chain.

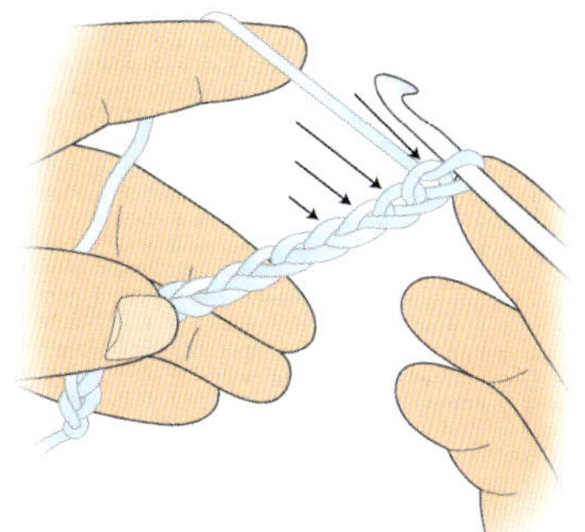

Magic ring

This is a useful starting technique if you do not want a visible hole in the center of your round. Loop the yarn around your finger, insert the hook through the ring, yarn over hook, pull through the ring to make the first chain. Work the number of stitches required into the ring and then pull the end to tighten the center ring and close the hole.

Enclosing a yarn tail

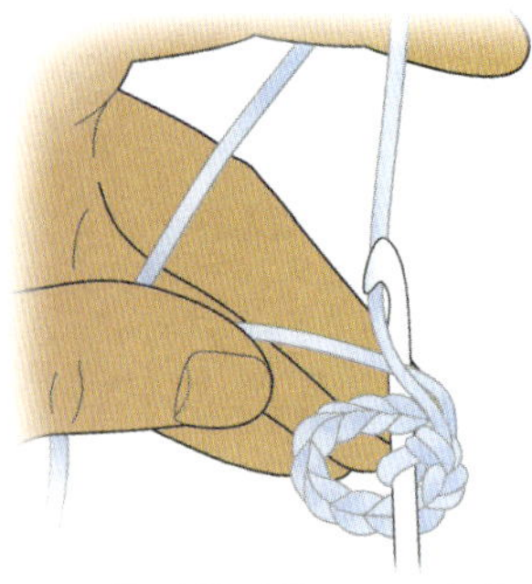

You may find that the yarn tail gets in the way as you work; you can enclose this into the stitches as you go by placing the tail at the back as you wrap the yarn. This also saves having to sew this tail end in later.

Slip stitch (sl st)

A slip stitch doesn't create any height and is often used as the last stitch to create a smooth and even round or row.

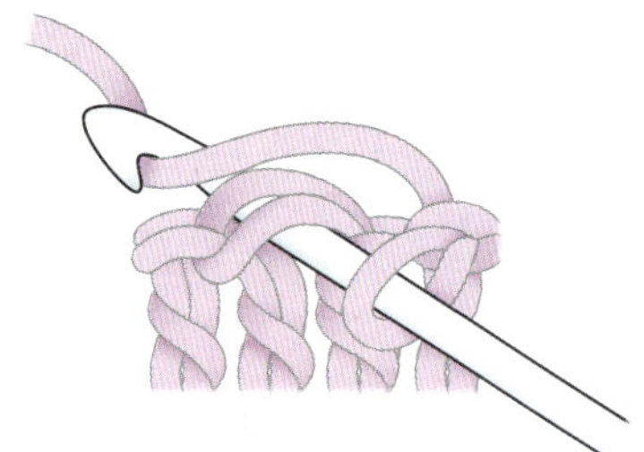

1 To make a slip stitch: first put the hook through the work, yarn over hook.

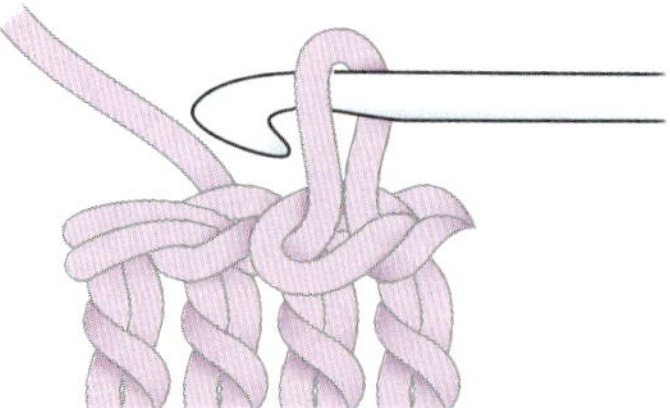

2 Pull the yarn through both the work and through the loop on the hook at the same time, so you will have 1 loop on the hook.

Making rounds

When working in rounds the work is not turned, so you are always working from one side. Depending on the pattern you are working, a "round" can be square. Start each round by making one or more chains to create the height you need for the stitch you are working:

Single crochet = 1 chain
Half double crochet = 2 chains
Double crochet = 3 chains
Treble = 4 chains
Double treble = 5 chains

Work the required stitches to complete the round. At the end of the round, slip stitch into the top of the chain to close the round.

Continuous spiral

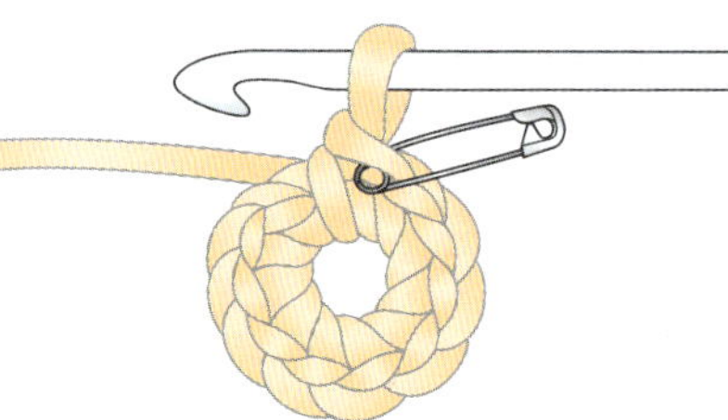

If you work in a spiral you do not need a turning chain. After completing the base ring, place a stitch marker in the first stitch and then continue to crochet around. When you have made a round and reached the point where the stitch marker is, work this stitch, take out the stitch marker from the previous round and put it back into the first stitch of the new round. A safety pin or piece of yarn in a contrasting color makes a good stitch marker.

Making rows

When making straight rows you turn the work at the end of each row and make a turning chain to create the height you need for the stitch you are working with, as for making rounds.

Single crochet = 1 chain
Half double crochet = 2 chains
Double crochet = 3 chains
Treble = 4 chains
Double treble = 5 chains

Joining a round with slip stitch

When working in rounds, or when adding an edging around a piece worked in rows, for a neat finish you will have to join the end of the round to the beginning with a slip stitch. You will be instructed in the pattern where to place the hook to work the slip stitch.

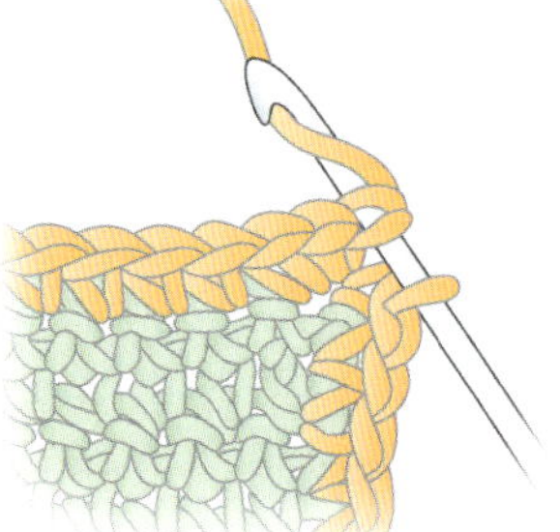

1 Work the round, which here is a single crochet edging. After completing the last stitch, insert the hook into the top of the first stitch and wrap the yarn over the hook.

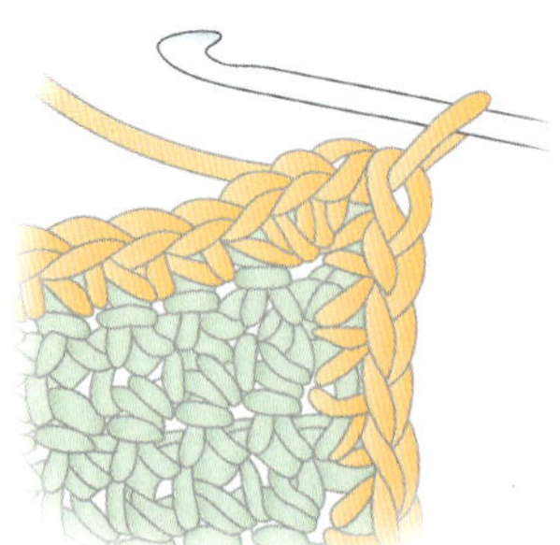

2 Pull the yarn through both the stitch and loop on the hook to join the 2 stitches (1 loop on hook). Fasten off the yarn as explained on page 124.

Working into top of stitch

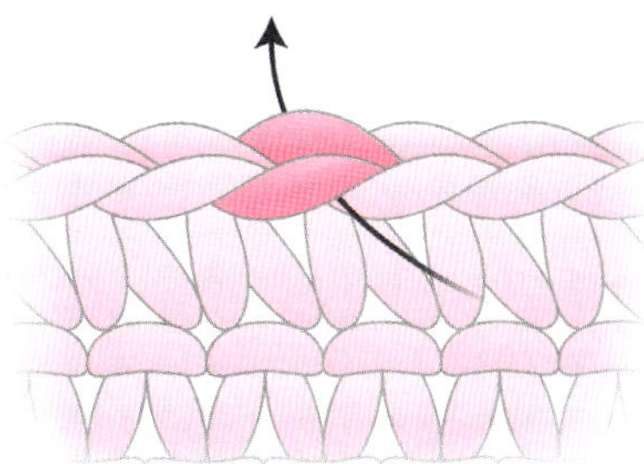

Unless otherwise directed, always insert the hook under both of the two loops on top of the stitch—this is the standard technique.

Working into front loop of stitch (FLO)

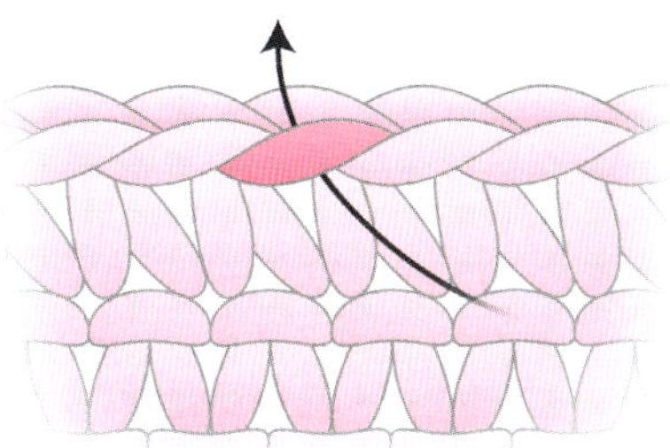

To work into the front loop of a stitch, pick up the front loop from underneath at the front of the work.

Working into back loop of stitch (BLO)

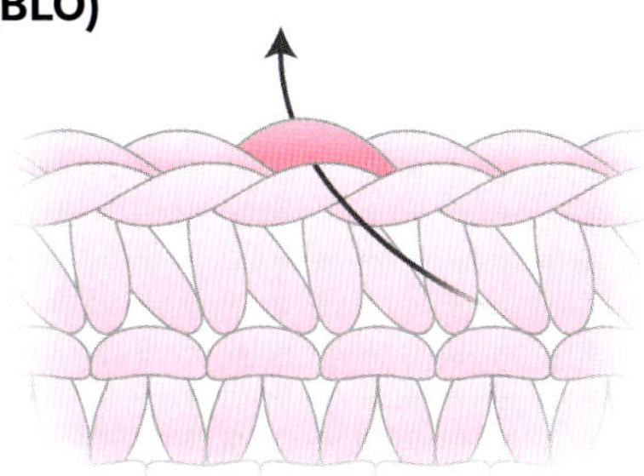

To work into the back loop of the stitch, insert the hook between the front and the back loop, picking up the back loop from the front of the work.

Working into a chain space

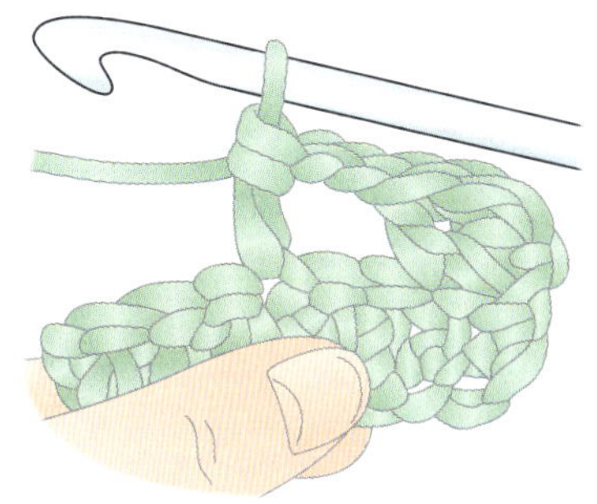

1 A chain space is the space that has been made under a chain in the previous round or row, and falls in between other stitches. It is abbreviated as "ch sp."

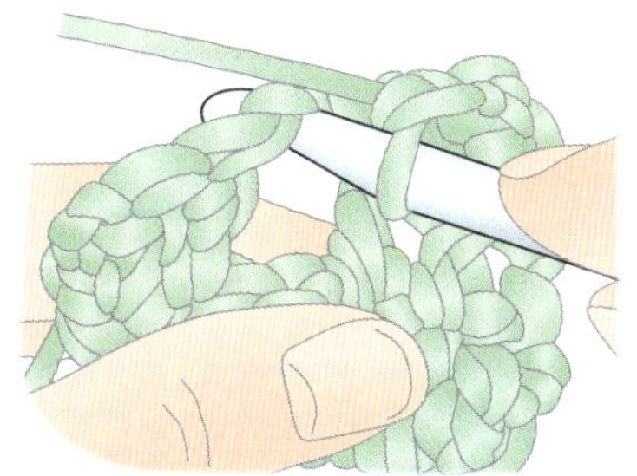

2 Stitches into a chain space are made directly into the hole created under the chain and not into the chain stitches themselves.

Single crochet (sc)

1 Insert the hook into your work, yarn over hook and pull the yarn through the work only. You will then have 2 loops on the hook.

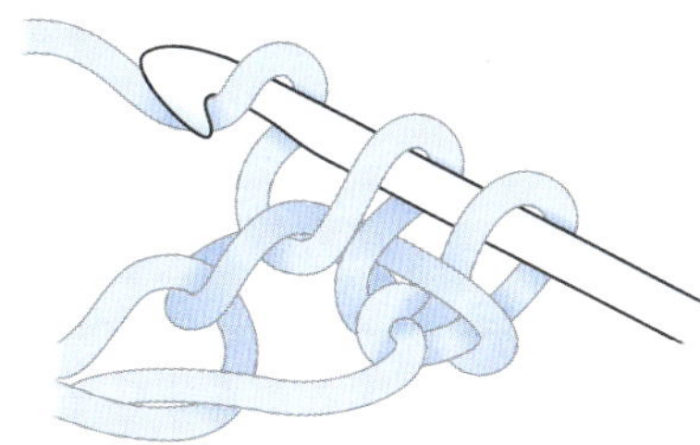

2 Yarn over hook again and pull through the 2 loops on the hook.
You will then have 1 loop on the hook.

Half double crochet (hdc)

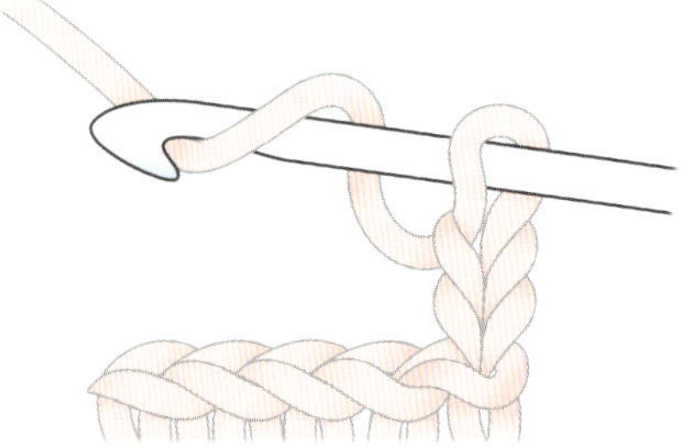

1 Before inserting the hook into the work, wrap the yarn over the hook and put the hook through the work with the yarn wrapped over.

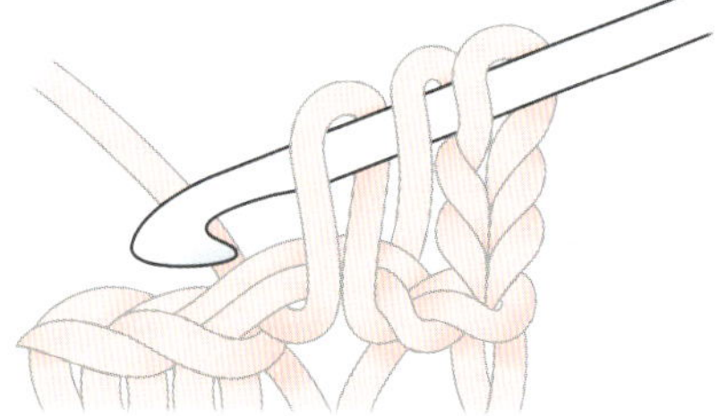

2 Yarn over hook again and pull through the first loop on the hook. You now have 3 loops on the hook.

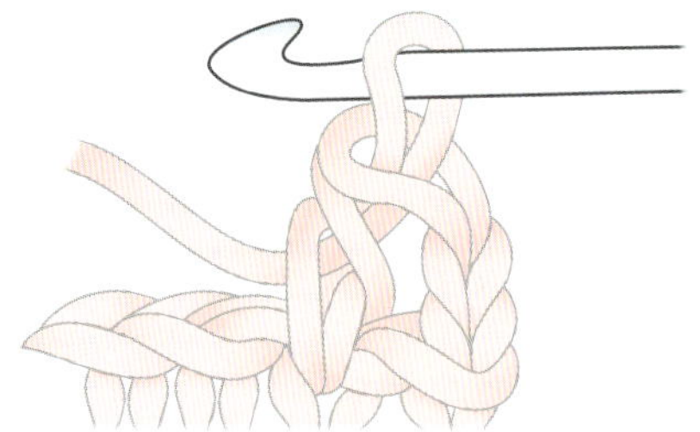

3 Yarn over hook and pull the yarn through all 3 loops. You will be left with 1 loop on the hook.

Double crochet (dc)

1 Before inserting the hook into the work, wrap the yarn over the hook. Put the hook through the work with the yarn wrapped over it, yarn over hook again and pull through the first loop on the hook. You now have 3 loops on the hook.

2 Yarn over hook again, pull the yarn through the first 2 loops on the hook. You now have 2 loops on the hook.

3 Yarn over, pull the yarn through 2 loops again. You will be left with 1 loop on the hook.

Treble crochet (tr)

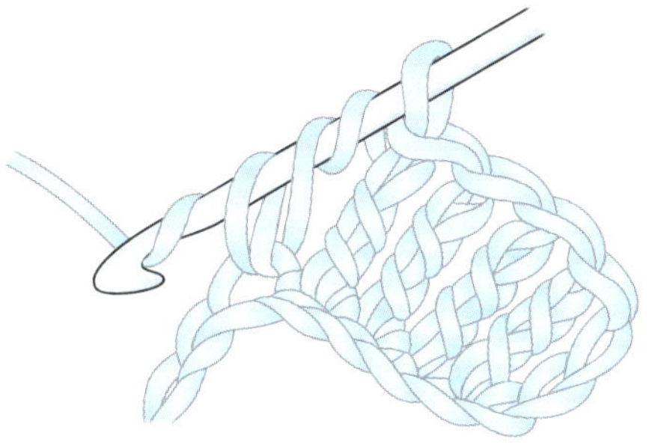

Yarn over hook twice, insert the hook into the stitch, yarn over hook, pull a loop through (4 loops on hook), yarn over hook, pull the yarn through 2 stitches (3 loops on hook), yarn over hook, pull a loop through the next 2 stitches (2 loops on hook), yarn over hook, pull a loop through the last 2 stitches. You will be left with 1 loop on the hook.

Double treble crochet (dtr)

Double trebles are 'tall' stitches and are an extension on the basic treble stitch. They need a turning chain of 5 chains.

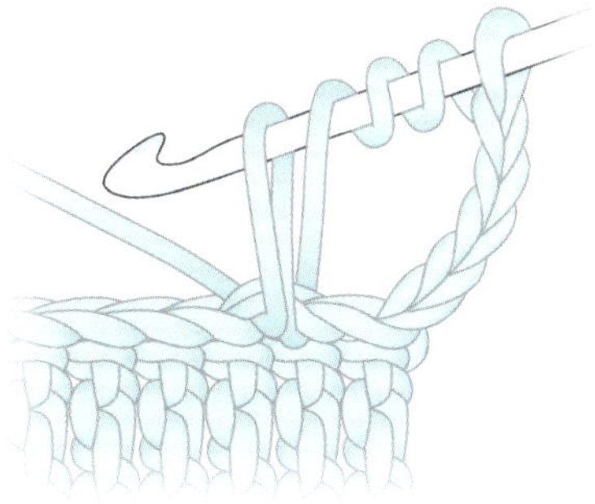

1 Yarn over hook three times, insert the hook into the stitch or space. Yarn over hook, pull the yarn through the work (5 loops on hook).

2 Yarn over hook, pull the yarn through the first 2 loops on the hook (4 loops on hook).

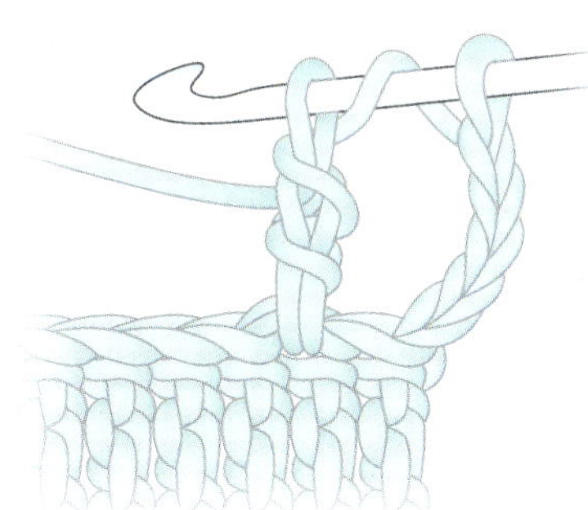

3 Yarn over hook, pull the yarn through the first 2 loops on the hook (3 loops on hook).

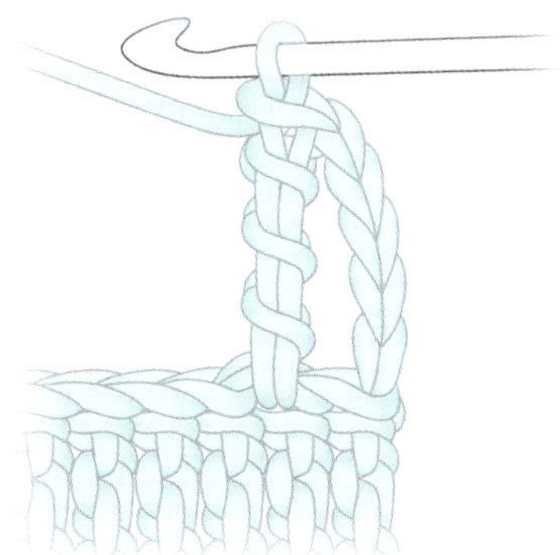

4 Yarn over hook, pull the yarn through the first 2 loops on the hook (2 loops on hook). Yarn over hook, pull the yarn through the 2 loops on the hook. You will be left with 1 loop on the hook.

Increasing

Make two or three stitches into one stitch or space from the previous row. The illustration shows a double crochet increase being made.

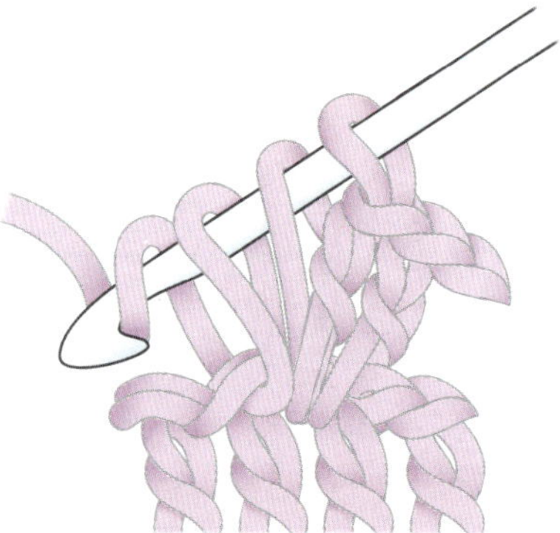

Decreasing

You can decrease by either missing the next stitch and continuing to crochet, or by crocheting two or more stitches together. The basic technique for crocheting stitches together is the same, no matter which stitch you are using. The following example shows sc2tog.

Single crochet two stitches together (sc2tog)

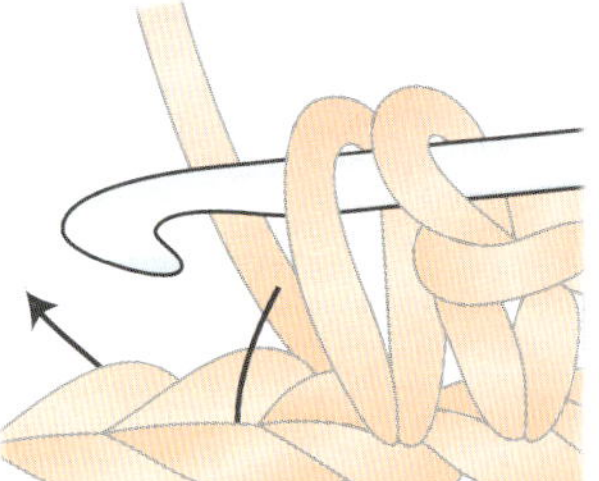

1 Insert the hook into your work, yarn over hook and pull the yarn through the work (2 loops on hook). Insert the hook in next stitch, yarn over hook and pull the yarn through.

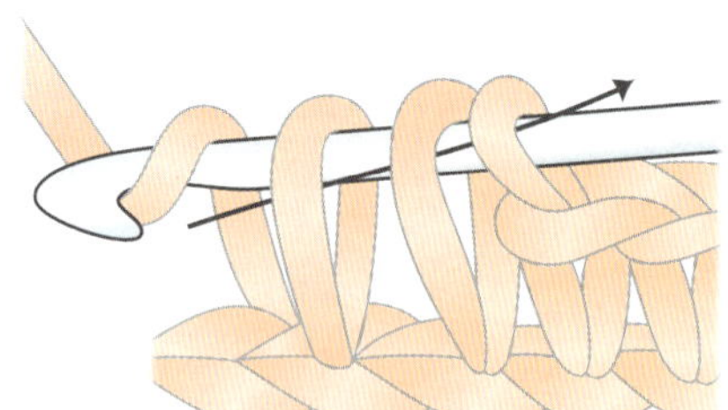

2 Yarn over hook again and pull through all 3 loops on the hook. You will then have 1 loop on the hook.

Three-double crochet cluster

Clusters are groups of stitches, with each stitch only partly worked and then all joined at the top to create a particular pattern or shape. They are most effective when made using a longer stitch, such as double crochet. This cluster is made up of three doubles and is abbreviated as '3dcCL'.

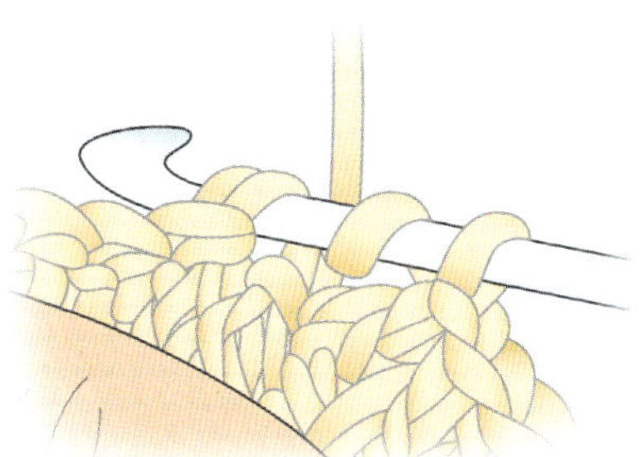

1 Yarn over hook, insert the hook in the stitch (or space).

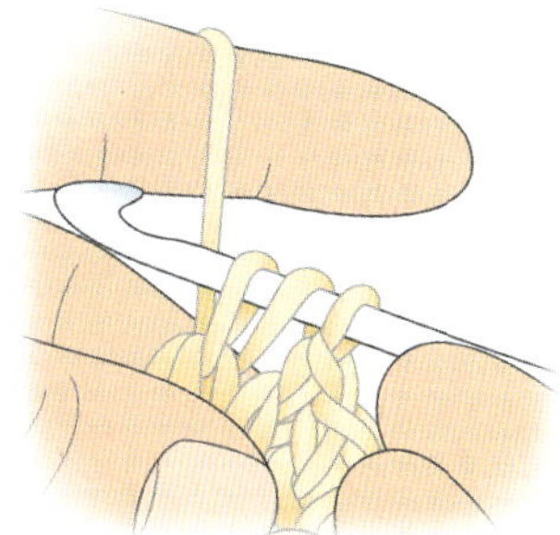

2 Yarn over hook, pull the yarn through the work (3 loops on the hook).

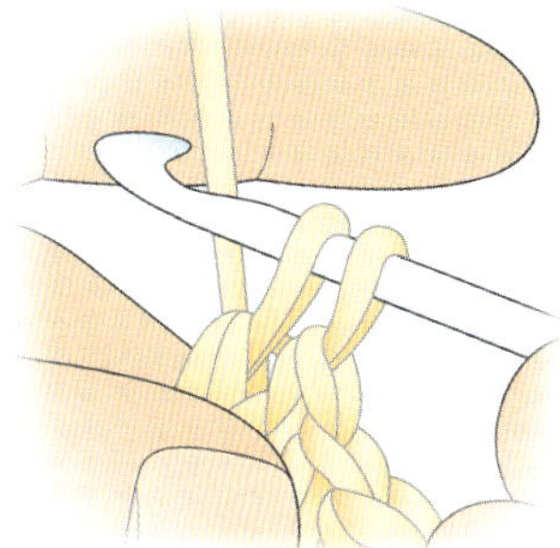

3 Yarn over hook, pull the yarn through 2 loops on the hook (2 loops on the hook).

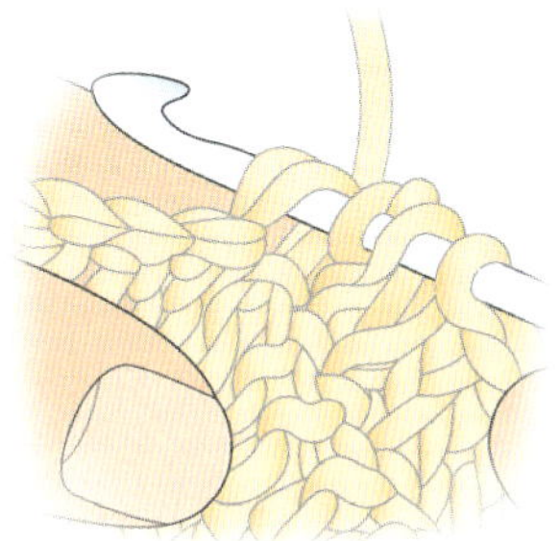

4 Yarn over hook, insert the hook in the same stitch (or space).

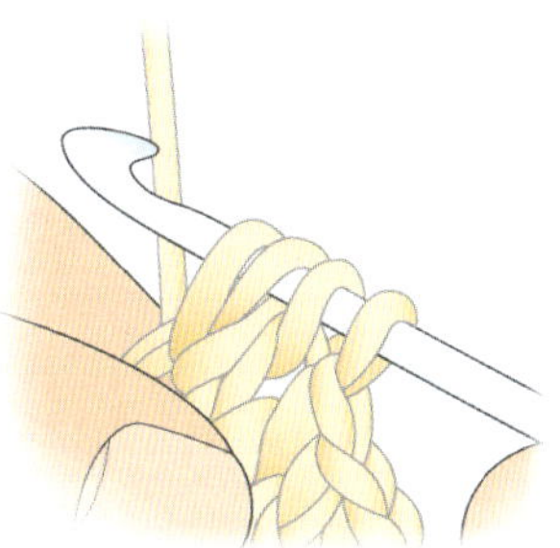

5 Yarn over hook, pull the yarn through the work (4 loops on the hook).

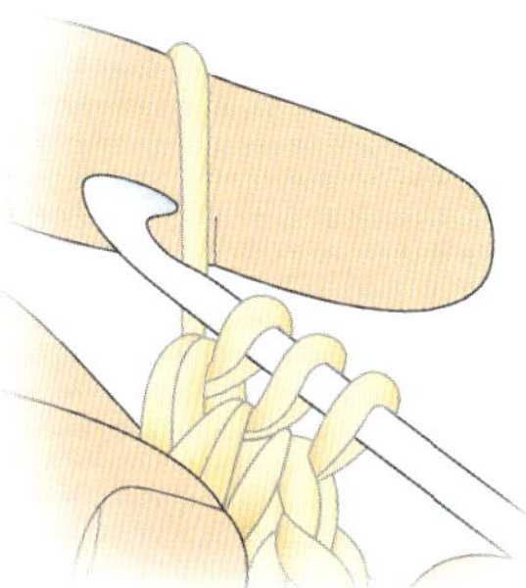

6 Yarn over hook, pull the yarn through 2 loops on the hook (3 loops on the hook).

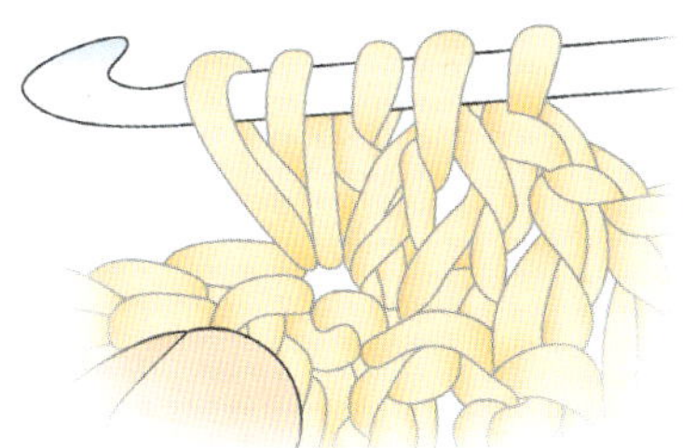

7 Yarn over hook, insert the hook in the same stitch (or space), yarn over hook, pull the yarn through the work (5 loops on the hook).

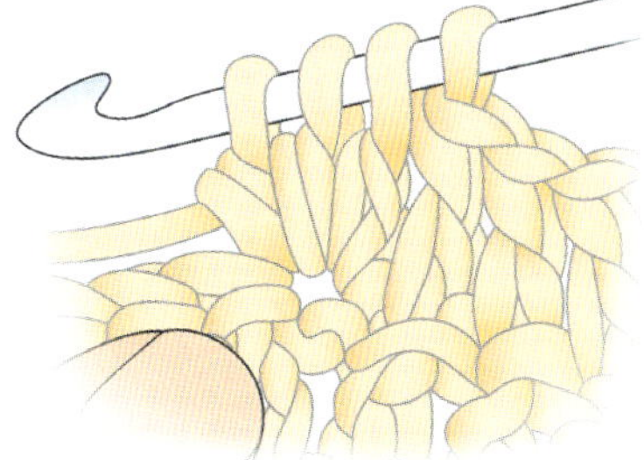

8 Yarn over hook, pull the yarn through 2 loops on the hook (4 loops on the hook).

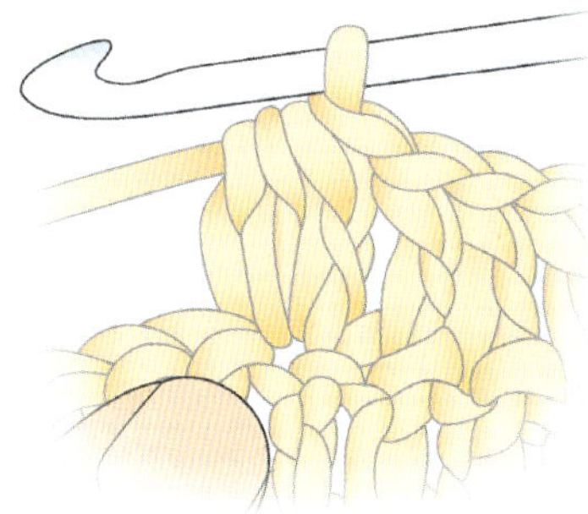

9 Yarn over hook, pull the yarn through all 4 loops on the hook (1 loop on the hook).

Standing single crochet

This is a neat, seamless method to join in a new yarn color or for the start of a new round.

1 Make a slip stitch and place it onto your hook.

2 Insert hook into the stitch.

3 Yarn over hook and pull through (2 loops on hook).

4 Yarn over hook and pull through to complete the stitch.

Joining yarn with a slip stitch

You can use this technique when changing color, or when joining in a new ball of yarn as one runs out.

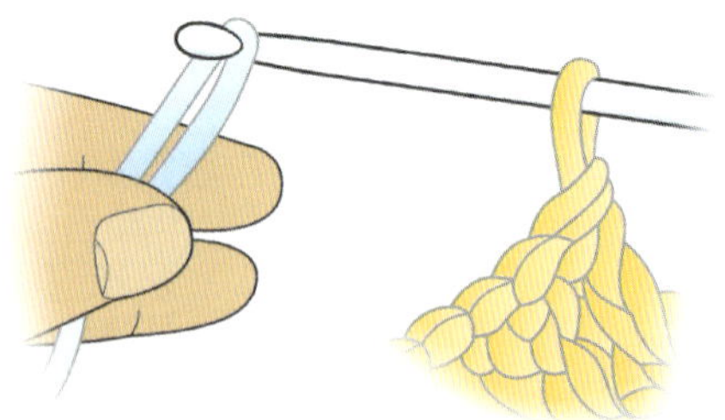

1 Keep the loop of the old yarn on the hook. Drop the tail and catch a loop of the strand of the new yarn with the crochet hook.

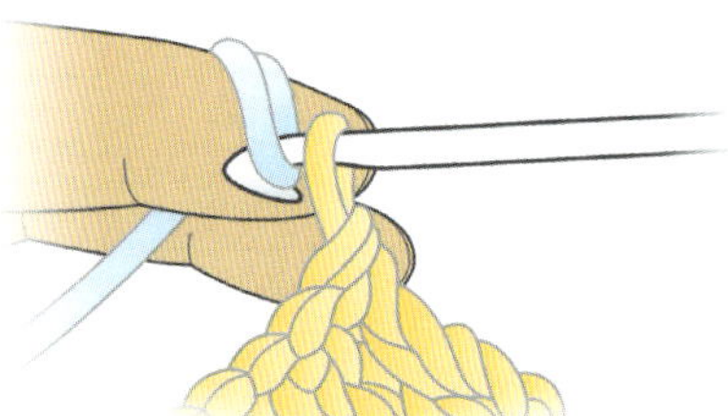

2 Draw the new yarn through the loop on the hook, keeping the old loop drawn tight and continue as instructed in the pattern.

Changing color in the middle of a row or round or on last yarn over hook

This method can be used to create a neat color join in the middle of a row or round, or on the last yarn over hook.

Joining a new color into single crochet

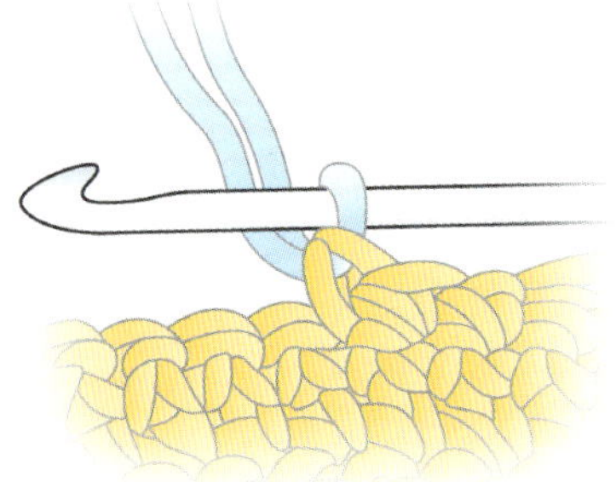

1 Make a single crochet stitch (see page 117), but do not draw the final loop through, so there are 2 loops on the hook. Drop the old yarn, catch the new yarn with the hook and draw it through both loops to complete the stitch and join in the new color at the same time.

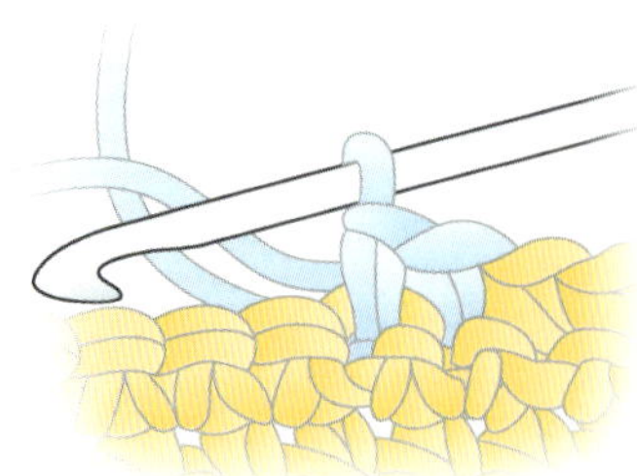

2 Continue to crochet with the new yarn. Cut the old yarn leaving a 6in (15cm) tail and weave the tail in (see page 124) after working a row, or once the work is complete.

Working over yarn along a row

Working over the yarn along a row involves carrying one or more additional colors through the work until you are ready to use them. It's the crochet equivalent of Fair Isle or stranding in knitting, but with the bonus that the second color is not visible at the back of the work—it is fully enclosed in the stitches of the first color. These steps show you how to do this in single crochet, but the same principle applies to whichever stitch you are using.

Joining a new color into single crochet

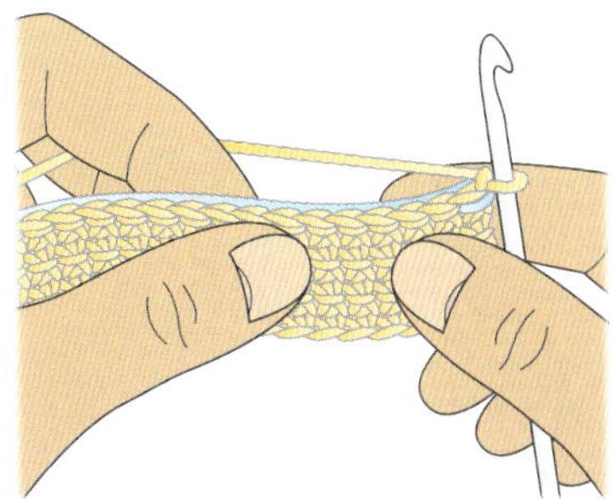

1 Hold the second color yarn along the top of the stitches from the previous row. You can do this from the beginning of a row, or join it a few stitches before you need to start using it, if it is only going to be used for a small area.

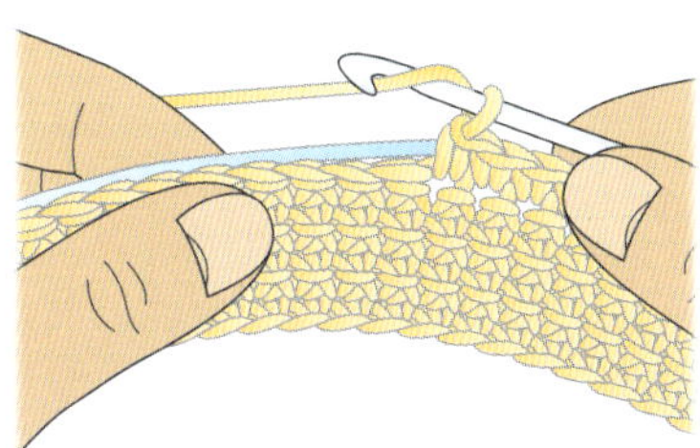

2 Work stitches in the normal way in the first color, but going over the second color and ensuring it is "trapped" within the stitches. Continue working in this way, carrying the second color until you are ready to work a stitch in it.

Changing color in single crochet

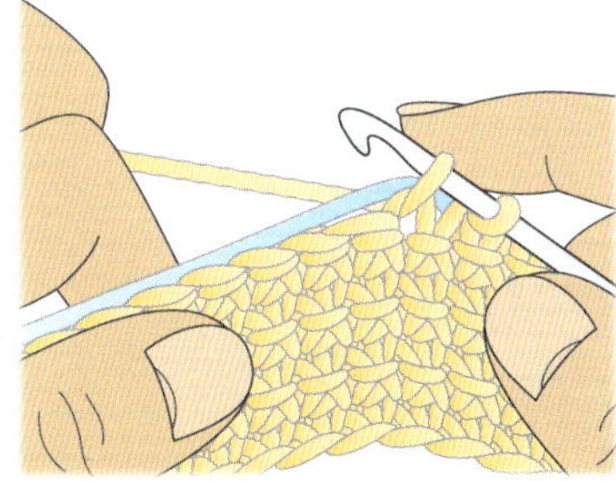

1 With the first color, pull the yarn through the next stitch, yarn over hook and pull through.

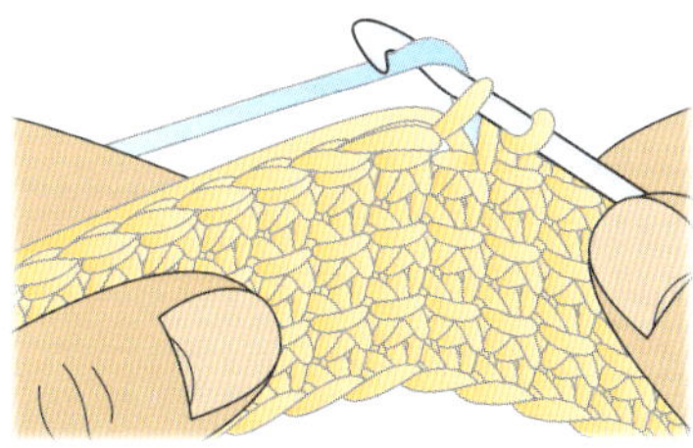

2 Using the second color, yarn over hook.

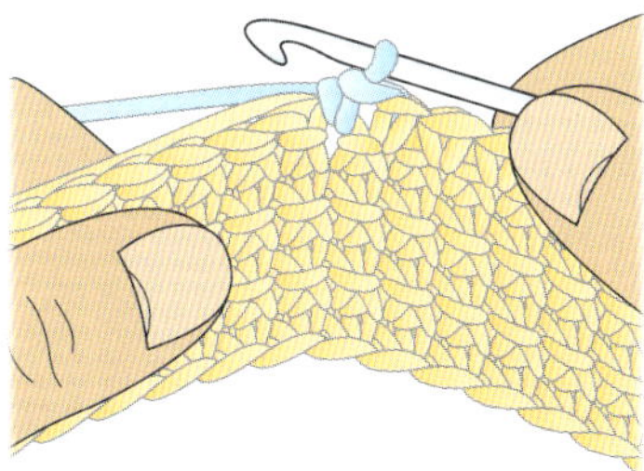

3 Pull the new color yarn through both loops on the hook to complete the stitch and change to the new color. Continue in the second color, working over the first color.

Turning at the end of a row

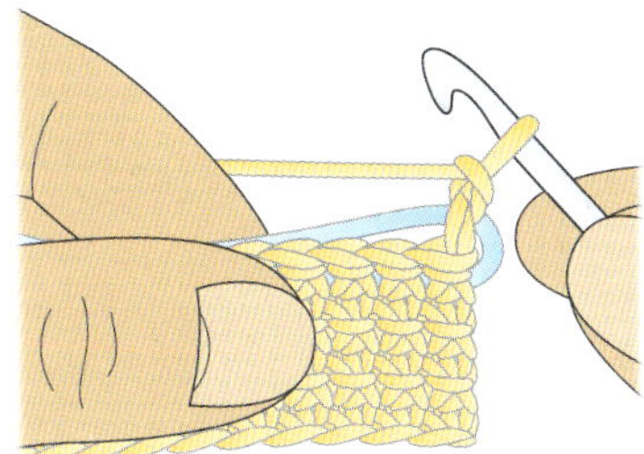

1 With the working color, make the appropriate length turning chain. Pull the second yarn up, holding it tight along the top of your work. Work the next stitch over the second yarn, catching it behind the piece.

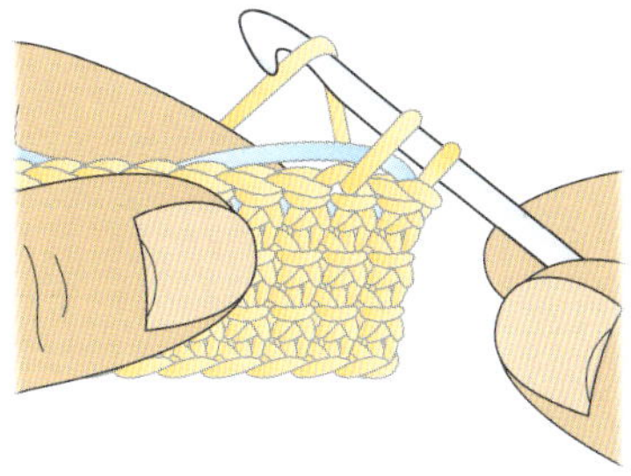

2 Continue to work over the second yarn as shown.

Fastening off

When you have finished crocheting, you need to fasten off the stitches to stop all your work unraveling.

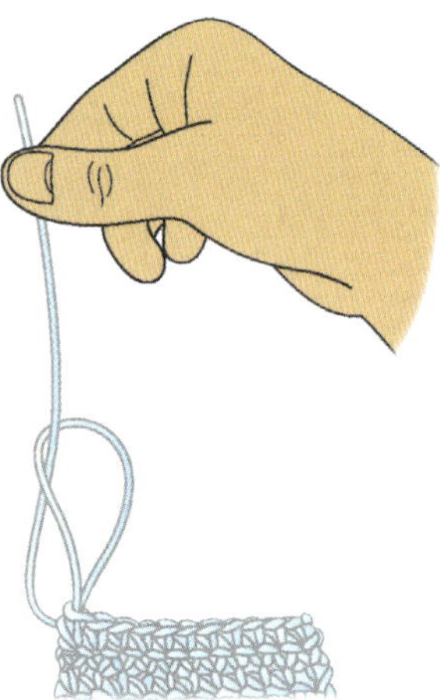

Draw up the final loop of the last stitch to make it bigger. Cut the yarn, leaving a tail of approximately 4in (10cm)—unless a longer end is needed for sewing up. Pull the tail all the way through the loop and pull the loop up tightly.

Weaving in yarn ends

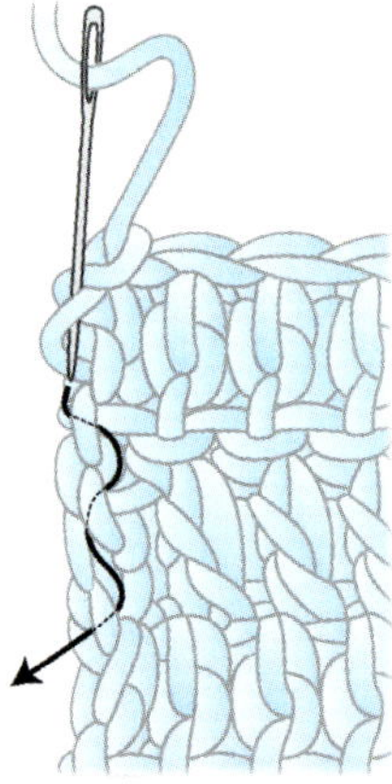

It is important to sew in the tail ends of the yarn so that they are secure and your crochet won't unravel. Thread a yarn needle with the tail end of yarn. On the wrong side, take the needle through the crochet one stitch down on the edge, then take it through the stitches, working in a gentle zig-zag. Work through four or five stitches then return in the opposite direction. Remove the needle, pull the crochet gently to stretch it and trim the end.

Blocking

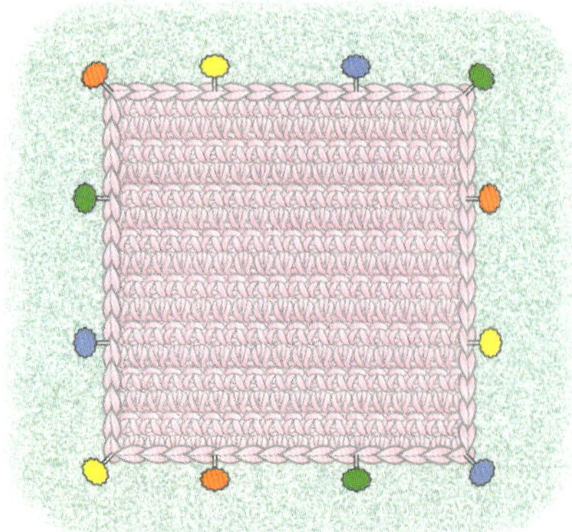

Crochet can tend to curl, so to make flat pieces stay flat you may need to block them. Pin the piece out to the correct size and shape on an ironing board or some soft foam mats (such as the ones sold as children's play mats). Spray the crochet with water and leave it to dry completely before unpinning and removing from the board or mats.

Joining pieces together

Making a single crochet seam or slip stitch seam

With a single crochet seam you join two pieces together using a crochet hook and working a single crochet stitch through both pieces, instead of sewing them together with a tail of yarn and a yarn sewing needle. This makes a quick and strong seam and gives a slightly raised finish to the edging. For a less raised seam, follow the same basic technique, but work each stitch in slip stitch rather than single crochet.

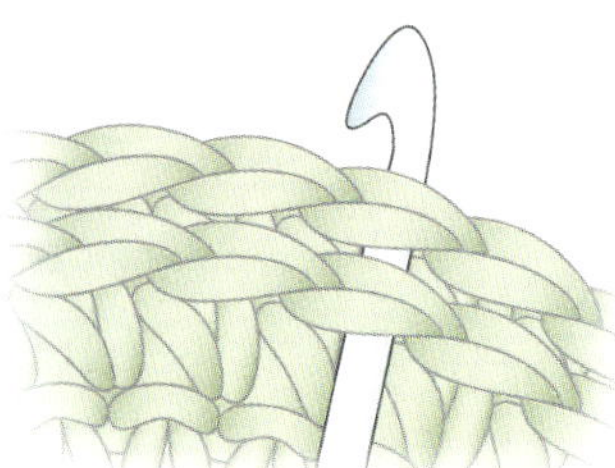

1 Start by lining up the two pieces with wrong sides together. Insert the hook in the top 2 loops of the stitch of the first piece, then into the corresponding stitch on the second piece.

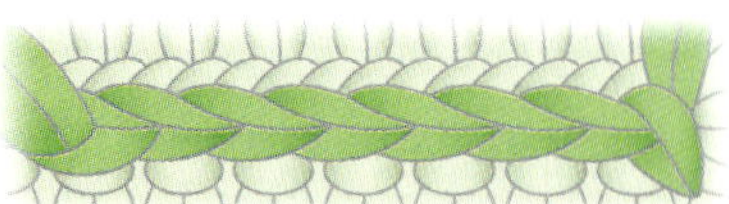

2 Complete the single crochet stitch as normal and continue on the next stitches as directed in the pattern. This gives a raised effect if the single crochet stitches are made on the right side of the work.

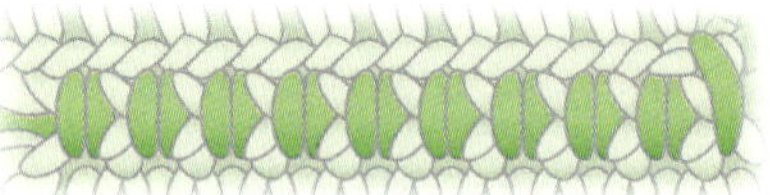

3 You can work with the wrong side of the work facing (with the pieces right side facing) if you don't want this effect and it still creates a good strong join.

Making an oversewn seam

An oversewn join gives a nice flat seam and is the simplest and most common joining technique.

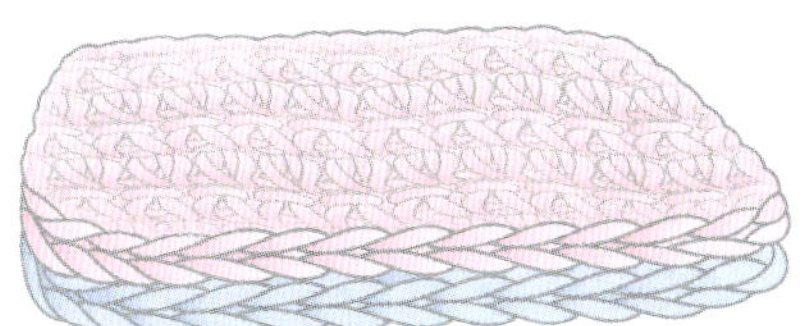

1 Thread a yarn needle with the yarn you're using in the project. Place the pieces to be joined with right sides together.

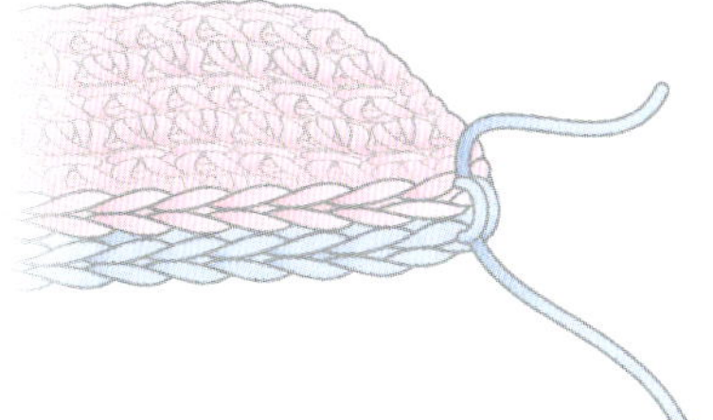

2 Insert the needle in one corner in the top loops of the stitches of both pieces and pull up the yarn, leaving a tail of about 2in (5cm). Go into the same place with the needle and pull up the yarn again; repeat two or three times to secure the yarn.

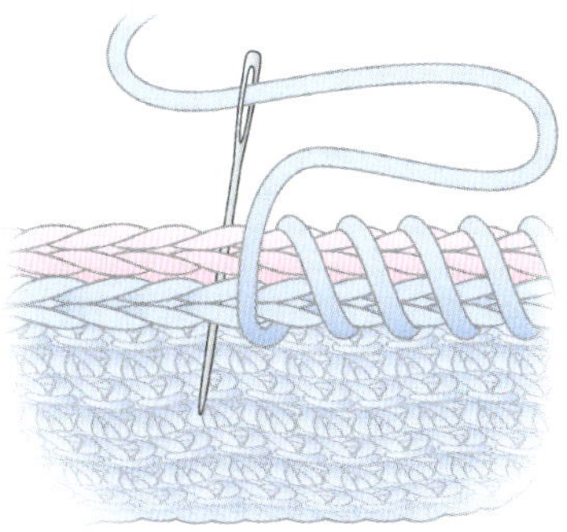

3 Join the pieces together by taking the needle through the loops at the top of the corresponding stitches on each piece to the end. Fasten off the yarn at the end, as in step 2.

Mattress/invisible seam

Using mattress stitch creates an invisible seam. It is made by picking up a loop or bar of the first crochet piece, and then picking up the bar from the corresponding stitch on the second piece. For the blocks and projects in this book, work through the back loops of the stitches only. This allows the front loops to align neatly on the surface, creating a clean finish and helping the blocks to lay flat.

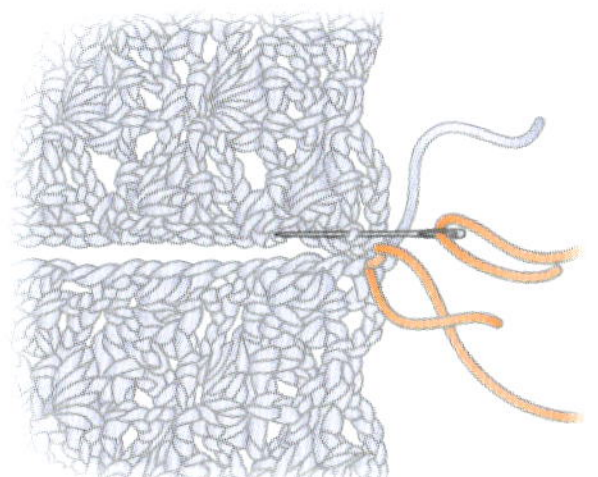

1 Line up the two pieces—pin them together if it helps make them more secure. Thread a tail of yarn in the same color as the pieces you're joining into a yarn sewing needle. Pick up the back loop of the stitch on the other side with the yarn sewing needle at a horizontal angle (90-degree angle) to the pattern and draw the yarn through loosely.

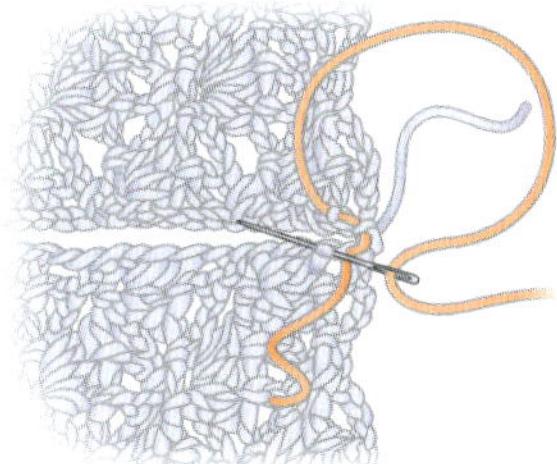

2 Pick up a back loop on the corresponding side of the other piece just inside the edge and draw through the yarn. Leave the loops loose and don't draw them through tightly.

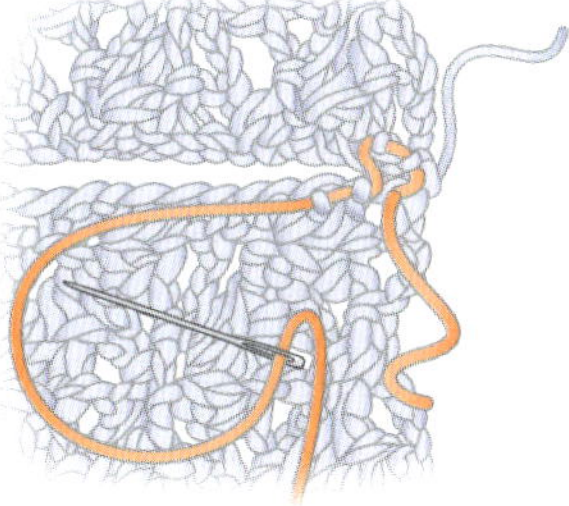

3 Pick up the next back loop approximately ½in (1cm) along on the same side and draw through the yarn.

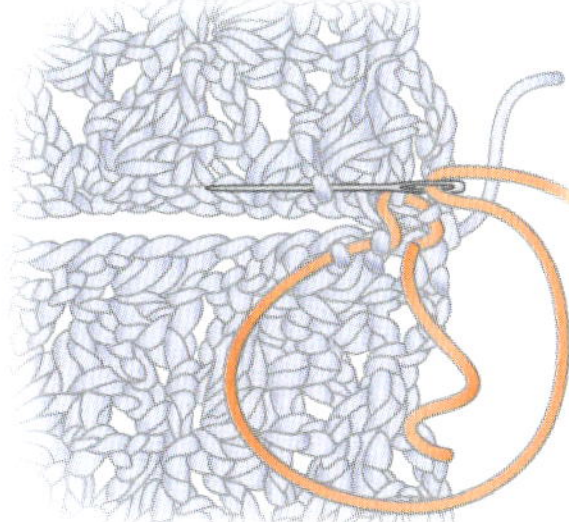

4 Pick up a back loop on the corresponding side of the other piece just inside the edge and draw through the yarn. Leave the loops loose and don't draw them through tightly.

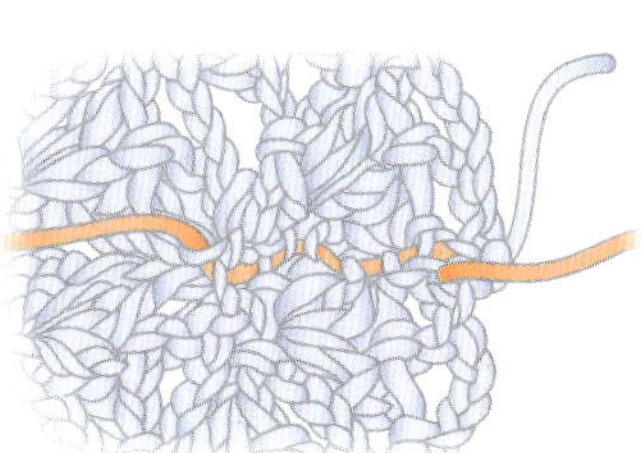

5 Repeat steps 3 and 4. When you have about 6 loops, hold the pieces firmly in place and pull the thread to draw the loose loops and bind the edging together.

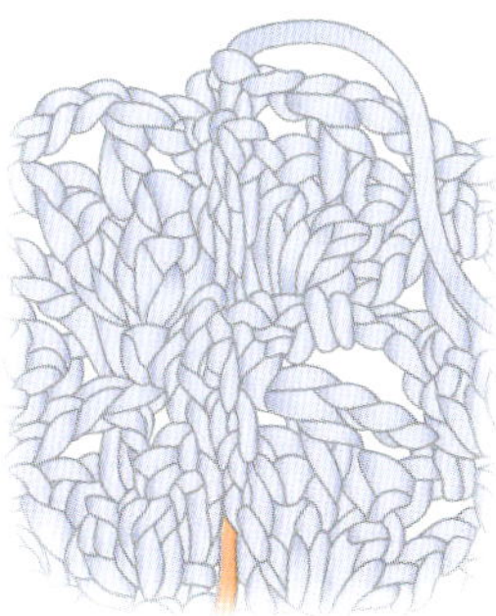

6 Continue in this way, repeating steps 3, 4 and 5 until the seam is joined. This will create an invisible seam on the right side of the work.

Abbreviations

beg – beginning
BLO – back loop only
ch – chain
cont – continu(e)ing
dc – double crochet
dc2tog – double crochet 2 stitches together
dtr – double treble
hdc – half double
rep – repeat
RS – right side
sc – single crochet
sl st – slip stitch
sp – space
st(s) – stitch(es)
tr – treble crochet
WS – wrong side
yoh – yarn over hook
( ) – stitch sequences within round brackets are worked into the same stitch or space stated
[ ] – stitch sequences within square brackets are worked the number of times stated
* – repeat sequence from * number of times stated

Quilting abbreviations

HST – half square triangle
QST – quarter square triangle
SQST – split quarter square triangle

Crochet stitch conversion chart

Crochet stitches are worked in the same way in both the UK and the USA, but the stitch names are not the same and identical names are used for different stitches. Below is a list of the US terms used in this book, and the equivalent UK terms.

US TERM	UK TERM
single crochet (sc)	double crochet (dc)
half double (hdc)	half treble crochet (htr)
double crochet (dc)	treble crochet (tr)
treble (tr)	double treble (dtr)
double treble (dtr)	triple treble (ttr)
gauge	tension
yarn over hook (yoh)	yarn round hook (yrh)

Suppliers

We cannot cover all stockists here, so please explore the local yarn shops and online retailers in your own country. If you wish to substitute a different yarn for the one recommended in the pattern, try the Yarnsub website for suggestions: www.yarnsub.com.

USA

LoveCrafts
Yarn, hooks and craft supplies
www.lovecrafts.com

Knitting Fever Inc.
Yarn, hooks
www.knittingfever.com

WEBS
Yarn, hooks
www.yarn.com

Michaels
Craft supplies
www.michaels.com

UK

Groves
Yarn, hooks and craft supplies
www.grovesltd.co.uk

Hobbycraft
Yarn, hooks and craft supplies
www.hobbycraft.co.uk

John Lewis
Yarn, hooks and craft supplies
Telephone numbers of stores on website
www.johnlewis.com

Knit Pro
Hooks and accessories
www.knitpro.eu

Laughing Hens
Yarn, hooks
Tel: +44 (0) 1829 740903
www.laughinghens.com

LoveCrafts
Yarn, hooks and craft supplies
www.lovecrafts.com

Stylecraft
www.stylecraft-yarns.co.uk

Wool
Yarn, hooks
Store in Bath
+44 (0)1225 469144
www.woolbath.co.uk

Wool Warehouse
Yarn, hooks and craft supplies
Online sales
www.woolwarehouse.co.uk

Australia

Black Sheep Wool 'n' Wares
Yarn, hooks
Retail store and online
Tel: +61 (0)2 6779 1196
www.blacksheepwools.com

Sun Spun
Yarn, hooks
Retail store (Canterbury, Victoria) and online
Tel: +61 (0)3 9830 1609
www.sunspun.com.au

INDEX

Acknowledgments

To everyone who's picked up one of my books, made a project, shared a kind word or simply followed along—thank you. Your support has meant so much to me over the years. I feel truly grateful to be part of such a creative and generous community of makers, many of whom have become truly valued and inspiring friends.

A huge thank you to the tremendous and talented team at CICO Books for your continued belief in my work and for bringing these ideas to life so beautifully on the page.

And above all, to my husband, John, and our family—thank you for your constant support, patience, and encouragement every step of the way.